QUIVIRA SOCIETY
PUBLICATIONS

VOLUME V

ARNO PRESS

NEW YORK

1967

CHURCH OF NUESTRA SEÑORA DE LA PURÍSIMA CONCEPCIÓN DE ACUÑA

DIARY OF
THE ALARCÓN EXPEDITION
INTO TEXAS, 1718-1719

BY

FRAY FRANCISCO CÉLIZ

TRANSLATED BY

FRITZ LEO HOFFMANN

THE QUIVIRA SOCIETY

Los Angeles

1935

First Published by
THE QUIVIRA SOCIETY
1935

•

Republished by
Arno Press
1967

•

Library of Congress Catalog Card
Number: 67-24717

•

Manufactured in the U.S.A.
Arno Press Inc.
New York

CONTENTS

LIST OF PLATES

PREFACE

WHEN in January, 1933, the diary of the Alarcón expedition into Texas and Louisiana was found in the Archivo General de la Nación by Mr. Luis Ceballos and Miss María Viamonte, paleographers in the archives, it was not until the document was shown to the noted Mexican historian and scholar, Ing. Vito Alessio Robles, that its full importance came to be known. Ing. Alessio Robles, being an authority on the early history of northern Mexico and Texas, immediately had several transcript copies made of the manuscript, one of which he gave to me with the suggestion that I translate the document and have it published with notes. In accordance with his wishes, I have translated the diary, consulting the transcript and the original in the archives, and have made the notes with the aid of other historical manuscripts furnished me in the Archivo General and by using the historical works so generously lent me by Ing. Alessio Robles.

The diary, lost for more than two centuries, had been misplaced in an *expediente* entitled *Medidas de Tierras efectuadas en las Misiones de San Bernardino de la Candela y Santiago de Valladares, 1718* (*Survey of Lands effected at the Missions of San Bernardino de la Candela and Santiago de Valladares, 1718*), at the end of volume 360 of the section of the archives known as *Tierras*. In the meantime Señor Alessio Robles has published the original Spanish text, without notes, in the review, *La Universidad de México,* Tomo V, Nos. 25–26 (Noviembre–Diciembre, 1932), pp. 48–69, and Tomo V, Nos. 27–28 (Enero–Febrero, 1933), pp. 217–239. Since the original manuscript was not discovered until January, 1933, it must be noted that both numbers of this

I

review appeared several months later, the November–December number appearing in February and the January–February number in March of 1933.

The original manuscript consists of twenty-six sheets, 15 x 21.5 cms., written on both sides in a small hand by the chaplain of the expedition, Fray Francisco Céliz, a priest of the mission of El Dulcísimo Nombre de Jesús de Peyotes in Coahuila. The document carries no title. Alarcón's son, Francisco de Alarcón, in a letter written July 19, 1719, attached to the diary, calls it *El Diario de la conquista y entrada a los Thejas* (*The Diary of the conquest and entrance to the Thejas*).

I wish to acknowledge full appreciation to the University of Texas and the E. D. Farmer International Scholarship Committee for the liberal financial aid given me in the making of this study in Mexico; to Ing. Vito Alessio Robles for suggesting the translation and for his constant help in getting this translation ready for publication; to Dr. Charles W. Hackett, of the University of Texas, for meticulously checking my account of the route of Alarcón on maps in Texas which were unavailable to me in Mexico; to Misses María Viamonte and Mercedes Osorio and Mr. Luis Ceballos for the many kindnesses shown me in the Archivo General de la Nación in Mexico City; to Dr. Carlos E. Castañeda, of the University of Texas, for helpful suggestions and corrections made in the translation; to Mr. Henry R. Wagner for arranging for the publication of this diary by the Quivira Society; and to Dr. George P. Hammond, of the University of Southern California, and Dr. F. W. Hodge, of the Southwest Museum, for their self-denying interest and assistance in guiding the manuscript through the press.

FRITZ L. HOFFMANN

Mexico, D. F.
March, 1934

INTRODUCTION

DURING the three centuries following the conquest of Mexico, the extension of Spanish jurisdiction on the North American continent was based on three underlying motives: (1) the search for gold and other resources that would bring wealth and position to the discoverer and increased revenues to the royal treasury; (2) the conversion of the natives, bringing them into the fold of the " Holy Mother Church "; and (3) the fear of foreign encroachment on lands already claimed but not yet occupied by Spain. In no other part of Spain's vast dominions in the New World can these motives behind Spanish expansion, especially the last, be better illustrated than in Texas.

Since Texas was only an outlying border province, knowledge of it was scarce. Accordingly, interest in the Indians and the natural resources of that region, although important, were secondary in the minds of Spanish authorities when they decided to occupy Texas, and the outstanding basis was the fear of foreign intrusion. Each of the steps leading to the final Spanish occupancy of Texas followed, therefore, an aggressive move on the part of France to take possession of the same territory or to trade therein. The reply to La Salle's attempted colonization of Espíritu Santo bay in 1684–1689, took the form of a Spanish mission establishment in eastern Texas in 1690. When, in the last years of the seventeenth century, the point of international competition shifted to the coast of Florida and the mouth of the Mississippi, the Texas enterprise was abandoned, only to be resumed with the coming, in 1714, of a French trader, Louis de St. Denis, to the Spanish outposts on the Rio Grande. St. Denis' audacity resulted directly in the permanent occupancy by Spain of the eastern Texas region in 1716,

and indirectly in the settlement of the head of the San
Antonio river in 1718, the colony on the San Antonio
river being designed to act as an intermediate point on
the long route between the establishments in eastern
Texas and those on the Rio Grande and as a defense
against any further French designs on the Matagorda
bay region. This introduction will present a brief résumé
of the Spanish interest in Texas from 1519 to 1718.[1]*

The first white man known to set eyes on any part of
present Texas was Alonso de Pineda, who, sent out by
Francisco de Garay, governor of Santiago (Jamaica),
skirted the Gulf coast from Florida to Vera Cruz and
back in the same year that another Spaniard, Hernán
Cortés, was beginning his historic conquest of Mexico.
The territory thus roughly explored by Pineda was given
the name Amichel and granted in 1521 to Garay to be
settled. Garay's agents met only disaster in their colonizing attempts, and in 1523 Garay himself, after personally leading a colonizing expedition in which he came into
open conflict with Cortés, died as a captive in Mexico
City.

The pretentious and yet remarkable expeditions and
accompanying experiences of Pánfilo de Narváez and
Cabeza de Vaca (1528–1536), of Hernando de Soto and
Luis de Moscoso (1539–1543), and of Francisco Vás-
quez de Coronado (1540–1542) gave Spain little more
than claims to the northern regions of her great western
empire. The failure or ultimate ruin of these great explorers caused Spain to be content with merely asserting
these claims and to insist upon them only on the threat of
foreign encroachment in the territory explored. With the
exception of Florida (settled in 1565 as a counteraction
to French activity in that region) and New Mexico (occupied in 1598), little thought was given by Spain to

* See the notes at the close of the Introduction.

CHURCH OF SAN ANTONIO DE VALERO, "THE ALAMO"

populate these vast regions, and no other permanent settlements were made by her within the present limits of the United States until after the close of the sixteenth century. Until that time, the northern limit of settlement of New Spain, with the exception of Florida and New Mexico, extended roughly in a line drawn from the lower Rio Grande region to the Gulf of California.

The Spanish occupancy of the southwestern part of the present United States was the result of a gradual northward movement from the conquest made in central Mexico, a movement accentuated by recurrent tales of the discovery of fabulous riches in those regions or by fear of the encroachment of a foreign nation on the soil of New Spain. This northward advance of the Spaniards had, by 1562, reached such a point that the province of Nueva Viscaya was formed of the region which today comprises the states of Sinaloa, Durango, Chihuahua and the southern portions of Sonora and Coahuila. East of this the province of Nuevo León was created, in 1579, extending from the eastern limits of Nueva Viscaya to the Gulf of Mexico and as far south as present Tampico. In 1625, Martín de Zavala became governor of Nuevo León and with his administration began the real development of that region. However, the rapid expansion into the unsettled districts, the opening of new mines and the establishment of new towns brought about open boundary disputes between the provincial governments of Nuevo León and Nueva Viscaya. To settle these disputes and to control more effectively the hostile Indians between the two provinces, the *alcaldía mayor* of Nueva Estremadura was established in 1674 in the territory north of Saltillo. With the further development of this new district, it was created a province in 1687 and named San Francisco de Coahuila, being on an equal basis with Nuevo León and Nueva Viscaya. The town of Santiago de Monclova was made the capital of the new province thus formed, and Alonso de León the younger became its first governor.

The religious development of Coahuila went hand in hand with its political development. Indeed in certain portions of the province Franciscan missionaries from the newly founded College of Santa Cruz de Querétaro [2] were pushing far ahead of the civil settlements. By 1703 several important missions had been founded by these fathers on the Rio Grande itself, and for the protection of these missions the presidio of San Juan Bautista del Rio Grande [3] had been established in 1702. (This group of missions became the point of origin of most of the Spanish expeditions that entered Texas. The activities of the Queretaran fathers brought such renown and prosperity to their college that in 1706 several Queretarans founded the College of Nuestra Señora de Guadalupe in Zacatecas. [4] It was from these two apostolical colleges that most of the Franciscan fathers came who went to Texas.

Interest in Texas, however, was to develop first in another portion of New Spain. It is not known how early the first news was received by the Spaniards in New Mexico of the Indians known as Texas, but as early as 1630, Father Alonso de Benavides, in charge of the missions of New Mexico, suggested a direct means of communication from New Mexico to the Gulf coast by way of the fabulous and visionary kingdoms of Gran Quivira and of the Aijado Indians. To these two imaginary kingdoms was soon added that of the Great Kingdom of the Texas. [5] In 1650, an expedition from New Mexico, led by Captains Martín and Castillo, visited some Indians named Jumano in the region near present San Angelo, Texas. There, on the Concho river, a branch of the Colorado, they gathered pearls which four years later became the basis for another expedition to the same region. The pearls proved to be of little value, but trade was continued in buffalo skins and pecans. For these articles regular trips were made from New Mexico, and thus western Texas became well known to the Spaniards. With the Pueblo Indian revolt of 1680, the Spaniards had to fall back to their settlement at El Paso (present Juárez, Mexico). As a result, for several years the expeditions to the Jumano Indians were foregone. In 1683, however, a Jumano Indian appeared before the Spanish governor at El Paso to ask that the trade with his people be renewed. At the same time he told the governor of the *Gran Reyno de los Texas,* situated about fifteen days' journey east of his home. In their dealings with the Jumanos, the Spaniards had frequently heard of this " great kingdom," but now new and seemingly reliable information concerning the region had been received. This new kingdom, so the Indian said, was adjacent to Gran Quivira, and the people of the two districts exchanged frequent visits. To reach the one would mean to see the other. Such an opportunity could hardly be overlooked.

Accordingly, in 1683–1684, an expedition under Juan Domínguez de Mendoza and Father Nicolás López went to the villages of the Jumanos and penetrated that region as far east as present Ballinger, without finding the great kingdom dreamed of. Returning from central Texas, Mendoza and López continued on to Mexico City where they laid before the viceroy a plan to establish a settlement among the Jumanos. Before this plan could be approved, however, news reached New Spain of the bold encroachment of La Salle on the coast of Texas. The Jumano Indians were forgotten in the mad rush to find the foreigner and drive him from Spanish soil. The *Gran Reyno de los Texas* was to be reached not from the New Mexico settlements, but from the newly created province of Coahuila whose first governor, Alonso de León, was to be the first Spaniard to reach La Salle's ill-fated settlement.

At the time that Mendoza and López were preparing for their trip to the Jumano Indians, with hopes of arriving at the kingdom of the Texas, the Frenchman Robert Cavelier, Sieur de la Salle, after a triumphant descent of the Mississippi river to its mouth, was hurrying back to his king to place before him elaborate plans for colonizing northern New Spain. His ultimate aim was to establish a colony from which the French could easily introduce themselves into the northernmost Spanish settlements of New Spain, the main lure being the Spanish mines in northern Mexico. The time was opportune for such a project, for France and Spain were far from friendly and French buccaneers were playing havoc with the Spanish colonies in the Gulf of Mexico. The French king's consent to these plans was probably hastened by additional schemes to attack New Spain, such plots being presented to the French court at the same time by Diego de Peñalosa, a renegade Spaniard and former governor of New Mexico. Peñalosa had been before the French court from 1678 to 1684, and there can be little doubt that his project and La Salle's plans were closely related.

La Salle sailed from France with four hundred people in four vessels on July 24, 1684. On the way the Spaniards captured one ship, and in the following winter La Salle lost another while landing the colony on Matagorda bay. The sea commander of the expedition rebelled at the same time and returned to France in a third vessel, leaving the colony virtually stranded with but one ship, which also was finally lost in exploring the bay. Things went from bad to worse for the colonists, sickness and Indian attacks greatly thinning their ranks. La Salle soon moved the colony to a site at the head of Lavaca bay on the present Garcitas river,[6] where he built Fort St. Louis.

From there, owing to the increasing plight of the suffering colonists, he made four desperate attempts to reach the Mississippi river region where he could have met his subordinates coming to his relief from the Illinois country. On his fourth trip he was treacherously slain by one of his followers at a spot near modern Navasota. Most of the remaining colonists, who had already dwindled to only a few survivors, were massacred in a raid on the fort by the savage coast Indians early in 1689. In the years following, the Spaniards found a few survivors of La Salle's ill-starred colony in various parts of Texas.

The stir occasioned in Mexico over the news of the presence of Frenchmen on the Gulf coast, not far distant from the Coahuila settlements, can well be imagined. To expel the intruders a land expedition from Spanish Florida left for the west in 1686 in a vain attempt to reach the Frenchmen. From 1686 to 1688 five sea expeditions looking for La Salle explored the Gulf coast from Florida to Vera Cruz, to be rewarded only with finding the wrecks of La Salle's ships at Matagorda bay.

The first land expedition from the west seeking the French colony set out from Nuevo León in 1686 under De León and explored the south bank of the Rio Grande to its mouth. The next year and again in 1688, as governor of the new province of Coahuila, he crossed the river twice. On his third trip he succeeded in taking a Frenchman, who, although he had probably drifted down from the northeast and knew very little of La Salle's colony, was nevertheless ruling a tribe of Indians north of the Rio Grande. This discovery demanded action and De León immediately set out on another expedition, on which he finally found the remains of La Salle's fort in April, 1689, only a short time after it had been destroyed by the Indians.[7]

De León had found the French fort in ruins, it was

true, but the danger of further French encroachments still remained. Indeed, among the Indians living in the region of the destroyed fort, De León had found several Frenchmen, who were promptly sent to Mexico City. Toward the northeast, it was learned, the French had built another fort. The foreign menace would have to be dealt with immediately.

At this time a splendid opportunity presented itself to De León to help him in making a heroic plea for a settlement in Texas. A chief of one of the Texas tribes visited him while on the expedition, asking him for a mission among his people, the Nabedaches,[8] who lived farther to the northeast. The unusual attributes and virtues of this chief impressed De León's chaplain, Fray Damián Massanet, who vigorously seconded De León's suggestion. The consent of the Spanish authorities in New Spain was obtained, and the dream of finding the kingdom of the Texas was at last to come true.

|Accordingly, in 1690, De León, on his fifth expedition and accompanied by Massanet, visited the region of the Texas Indians, and among the Nabedache tribe of the Texas he founded two missions.| San Francisco de los Texas, the first Spanish mission in Texas, he placed near the Neches river in May, 1690.[9] The other he founded a few miles to the north and named it Santísimo Nombre de María.[10] The land occupied by the Indians of the Hasinai or Texas confederation now received the status of a province, with Domingo Terán de los Ríos as its first governor. Terán, in keeping with his title, in 1691 made an expedition to the Neches and Red rivers, accompanied by Father Massanet, but he succeeded in doing little more than changing the names of the places De León had visited and in having violent quarrels with Massanet. He soon returned to Mexico, leaving Massanet with two other friars and nine soldiers among the Indians.[11] The

missions survived only two more years. ｜The excitement
of the first moments of the French intrusion soon wore
off and with it disappeared the necessity of any posts on
the frontier. The much heralded kingdom of the Texas
had proved to be a disappointment, and, indeed, the Indians were daily becoming more hostile. Disease and
several crop failures finally added greatly to the obstacles
met by the missionaries, and on the night of October 25,
1693, the missions were abandoned, Massanet himself ap-
plying the torch to the building that had served as the
first mission in Texas.[12]

The danger of foreign encroachment had only been
temporarily shifted to another portion of Spain's over-
seas empire. The English in the Carolinas were reported
to have become interested in the tribes living to the
southwest of them and to be making incursions into
Spanish territory. Moreover, reports from France veri-
fied the fear that the French were planning to occupy
Pensacola bay in Spanish Florida. To counteract this
foreign aggression on her soil, Spain again acted in time.
Accordingly, a few months before the abandonment of
the Texas missions, Carlos de Sigüenza sailed from Vera
Cruz to explore the bays of Pensacola and Mobile and
the mouth of the Mississippi, but it was not until November, 1698, that Spain finally settled Pensacola.

The fortification of Pensacola bay had come none too
soon, for two months after the Spaniards had installed
themselves there, the French colonizer, Sieur d'Iberville,
appeared at the mouth of the bay. Finding it occupied by
the Spaniards, he moved on to Biloxi bay, where he established his settlement, thus taking permanent possession
of Louisiana for France. In 1710 the post was moved to
the present site of Mobile by Sieur de Bienville, brother
of Iberville. But the colony did not flourish, and, in 1710,
the French king, in order to rid himself of a white ele-

phant, granted a fifteen-year trade monopoly in Louisiana
to the wealthy French merchant Antoine Crozat, naming
at the same time La Mothe Cadillac, the founder of
Detroit, as the first governor of Louisiana. During
Cadillac's administration several groups of colonists were
sent to Louisiana. Still the colony would not prosper, and
as a final resort Cadillac decided to open a trade with
New Spain. An attempt by way of Vera Cruz having
failed, he resolved on an overland route to the Spanish
settlements on the Rio Grande. Again French intruders
were to menace Texas, and Spain again was to rise to
the occasion.

Governor Cadillac's opportunity came sooner than
even he had hoped for. At the Spanish missions on the
Rio Grande at that time lived a fervent missionary
named Francisco Hidalgo. Hidalgo had been among the
Texas Indians with Massanet and he longed to return to
his former wards. Being denied permission by his su-
periors, he conceived the idea of using the French menace
to accomplish his designs. Accordingly, in 1711 and 1712,
he wrote two letters to the French governor of Louisiana
asking him to aid the Texas Indians against their enemies
and to see to their welfare in general. After a long delay,
the first letter reached Cadillac in May, 1713. He immediately selected his best agent, Louis Juchereau de St.
Denis, to do his bidding. St. Denis lost no time. In the
latter part of the same year he founded the post of
Natchitoches [13] on the Red river and spent the winter
trading with the Indians. Having discovered that Father
Hidalgo was not among the East Texas tribes, as he had
thought, on June 1, 1714, with three other Frenchmen
and twenty-five Indians, he set out on foot for the Spanish
outposts on the Rio Grande. He reached the presidio of
San Juan Bautista on July 18th, to find that Hidalgo had
gone to Querétaro; but he was cordially received by the

missionaries and Diego Ramón, captain of the presidio. Ramón, while entertaining St. Denis on the Rio Grande, sent secret messages to Mexico City, asking the viceroy what to do with him, and St. Denis, in turn, spent his time in wooing Captain Ramón's granddaughter whom he soon married.[14]

St. Denis' presence among the Spanish settlements on the Rio Grande once more aroused the Spanish authorities in Mexico, who decided on the reoccupancy of the country of the Hasinai confederacy as a protection against further French encroachment. Domingo Ramón, son of the captain at San Juan Bautista, was placed in charge of the new expedition, and St. Denis, having won the confidence of the Spaniards by marrying a member of the Ramón family and by expressing the desire of soon becoming a Spanish subject, was employed as convoy or guide. The expedition, consisting of sixty-five people, included nine friars and six women. Among the missionaries were Father Isidro Felix de Espinosa,[15] Father Antonio Margil de Jesús[16] and Father Hidalgo, who now realized the fruits of his labors. The expedition crossed the Rio Grande in April, 1716, and after almost two months of travel reached the Texas villages. On the other side of the Neches river and a few leagues farther inland from where De León and Massanet had founded it in 1690, Ramón and Espinosa on July 3, 1716, reestablished the mission of San Francisco de los Texas or Neches.[17] Four days later, in the village of the Hainai, the principal settlement of the Hasinai confederacy, they founded the mission of Nuestra Señora de la Purísima Concepción.[18] Owing to its strategic position, this mission became the headquarters of the missionaries of the College of Santa Cruz de Querétaro, with Father Espinosa as the president. It had supervision of the missions of San Francisco de los Texas and San Joseph de los Nazones, founded by Espinosa and Ramón on July 10, 1716.[19]

In the meantime the missionaries of the College of Guadalupe of Zacatecas were not idle. As soon as Margil arrived in East Texas, preparations were made to embark upon their missionary activities with zeal. On July 9, 1716, Ramón and Margil founded the mission of Nuestra Señora de Guadalupe de los Nacogdoches.[20] It was the first Texas mission of the College of Guadalupe of Zacatecas and Father Margil became its president. Under its supervision[21] were placed the missions of Nuestra Señora de los Dolores de los Ais[22] and San Miguel de los Adaes,[23] founded in 1717 by Margil. By the end of 1717 the Texas settlements could boast of six missions and a presidio of twenty-five soldiers, the presidio having been established in 1716 by Ramón about one league east of the mission of Purísima Concepción. It received the name of Nuestra Señora de los Dolores de los Texas.[24]

Spanish dominion in the region of the Texas Indians had now been reëstablished and it seemed as if the fruits of the endeavors of the missionaries would be great. Largely through the efforts of St. Denis[25] the Indians had received the Spaniards with open arms, the presence of women among the new settlers acting as an incentive for added confidence in the natives. However, difficulties soon arose. After the missions had been established and the newness of their position had worn off, Ramón and his companions seriously considered their situation. It was after all not a very pleasant one. The difficulty in establishing the new settlements came not in founding them but in maintaining them; the support of six new missions anywhere in New Spain would have been a great problem in the eighteenth century, but in their maintenance in East Texas there was the added obstacle of

CHURCH OF SAN JOSÉ Y SAN MIGUEL DE AGUAYO

their great distance from the nearest other Spanish settlements. Moreover, the friendly Indians might at any
time prove not so understanding. A command from St.
Denis and they would be at the Spaniards' throats. The
nearness of the French on the Red river worried the new
settlers greatly, for the Indians displayed many guns,
knives, clothes, and trinkets that the French had given
them. The obedience of the Indians, the missionaries
soon discovered, could be bought only by gifts, and the
Spaniards had hardly enough supplies for themselves.
They soon appealed to the viceroy for additional aid,
and in their representations gave full accounts of their
difficult position. In order to keep a settlement at such a
great distance from the nearest Spanish settlement,
Ramón decided that another twenty-five men would be
needed, and suggested that the salary of each soldier be
raised. The high freight rate in transporting goods from
Saltillo demanded this. In addition, an annual appropria-
tion of not less than six thousand pesos would be necessary for the work of the missionaries.[26]

The letters from Ramón and the missionaries in East
Texas arrived in Querétaro in September, 1716. The
guardian of the College of Santa Cruz, Fray Joseph
Diez, immediately resolved[27] to send them on to the
viceroy with the ablest missionary at hand, Fray Antonio
de Sanbuenaventura y Olivares. Olivares had been on
an expedition a short distance beyond the Rio Grande,
was acquainted with the country and the Indians living
in it, and, most important of all, had a definite plan to
present to the viceroy for the welfare of the Texas
missions.

Olivares lost no time in Mexico City. At the request of
the viceroy he put his plans in writing. He proposed to
transfer the mission of San Francisco Solano, which he
had founded in 1700 near the mission of San Juan

Bautista on the Rio Grande, to the San Antonio river.[28] Few of the Jarame Indians[29] with whom he had founded San Francisco Solano, remained in that mission, and these he would use to teach the Payaya,[30] Sana[31] and Pampoa Indians[32] on the San Antonio river. The Jarames already knew how to cultivate the soil and serve the missionaries. For the mission he would need ten soldiers, and he desired a few settlers if they could be spared. He closed the letter by giving in detail the supplies that would be needed by him and his companions in founding the mission.[33]

Before taking action on the suggestions of Olivares, the new viceroy, the Marqués de Valero, who had succeeded the Duque de Linares on August 16, 1716,[34] requested a complete report from his legal department on the Province of the Texas and suggestions for its' further occupancy. Two reports were sent to him on November 30, 1716, one signed by the *fiscal de haciènda,* and the other by the *fiscal* of the audiencia.[35] In reviewing the history of the province of Texas from 1689 to 1716, the reports stressed the menace of the French. In fact, at that very time they had received reports that men were being recruited in France to establish a large colony on the Mississippi for the sole purpose of opening a trade with the province of Texas.[36] Faith in St. Denis and his plans was entirely lost, a blind fear of the French suddenly seizing the Spanish authorities. Reports from East Texas had only confirmed this fear, for, according to Ramón, the French were introducing great quantities of merchandise among the Indians and, soon after their arrival in Texas, St. Denis himself had gone on to Mobile to obtain more goods to bring into New Spain.[37] Furthermore, while holding a position and receiving a salary from the Spanish viceroy, St. Denis had written the French governor at Mobile to take possession of Espíritu Santo

bay.[38] The purpose of such a settlement was no doubt to
gain control over the Indians of the coast and of the re- ✓
gion between the province of Texas and the Rio Grande,
thereby cutting off all communication between Mexico
and the Texas settlements. With such an advantage the
French could, at their will, destroy the missions recently
founded by Ramón and his companions in Texas. ✗

However, still another feature had to be considered.
Olivares in his reports [39] had described the Texas country, showing the great natural resources abounding there
and the considerable number of Indians roaming the
country. The Indians living on the banks of the San Antonio river alone he estimated at three or four thousand.[40]
The *dictámenes* found sufficient authority for carrying
forward the conversion of these Indians in the royal
decrees of 1690 and 1692 which provided especially for
the conquest of the province of the Texas Indians. The
conversion of the natives and the development of the
country could go hand in hand with the fortification of
the region against any further attempts of encroachment
by the French.

The *fiscales,* therefore, counseled the viceroy to accept
the opportune suggestions of Olivares; to allow him and
two missionaries of his choice to found a mission on the
San Antonio river; to found a presidio at the same place;
to occupy as soon as possible Espíritu Santo bay, the
presidio at San Antonio to protect the region until a fort
could be established on the bay; to found a mission among
the Cadodacho Indians [41] in order to develop a trade in
the beavers abounding in their country; to name Don
Martín de Alarcón, because of his proved ability and
great zeal in the service of the king, as the man to lead
the new expedition into Texas; and to give Alarcón, besides the soldiers and missionaries, a master carpenter, a

master mason, and a weaver to go along at the same salaries as those of the soldiers.[42]

Perhaps the most interesting suggestion of the *fiscal* was that of a possible overland line of communication to be established between Florida and Texas. The basis of this opinion was a letter written by Don Gregorio de Salinas, Spanish governor at Santa María de Galve in Florida, in which he told the viceroy of having made an alliance with an Indian chief who ruled fifty-eight tribes extending as far west and north as the region of the Texas Indians. By a thorough settlement of the Texas country and by converting the Indians of the fifty-eight tribes referred to by Salinas, a line of defense could be established against the French which would be an effective barrier. Furthermore, such a connection would assure for all time the food supplies for the Texas as well as the Florida establishments.[43]

The proposals set forth in the *dictámenes fiscales* were presented to a *Junta General,* assembled by the viceroy on December 2, 1716.[44] This *junta* accepted the proposals of the *fiscales* and in addition determined that Captain Ramón should be ordered immediately to set out from his presidio in East Texas and reconnoiter the country of the Natchitoches Indians, taking captive any Frenchmen he might find and destroying their post.

On December 7, 1716, the viceroy appointed Alarcón head of the new expedition into Texas, giving him the title of *Governador y Teniente de Capitán* of the province of Texas.[45] At the same time he ordered that Olivares be given the supplies necessary for the founding of his mission on the San Antonio river. Olivares was to be allowed ten soldiers for his proposed mission, eight of whom were to be taken from the presidio of San Juan Bautista and two from the presidio of Coahuila at Monclova. Four or six of these soldiers were to reconnoiter the bay of Espíritu Santo at least once a month after the presidio on the San Antonio river was once established, and report anything unusual they might encounter.[46]

Very little is known of Martín de Alarcón's early life. What is known is based entirely on one document, dated January 18, 1721, which gives a glowing account of his earlier accomplishments with the ultimate purpose of his receiving an emolument from the Spanish king.[47] According to this document Alarcón recruited a company of infantry in Valencia, Spain, and was a soldier of fortune, serving in Orán and later in the royal Spanish navy. On May 31, 1691, he was named sergeant-major of the militia[48] of Guadalajara in New Spain. Soon thereafter he became *alcalde mayor* and captain of Jacona and Zamora, both places being in the present state of Michoacán, Mexico. On September 11, 1696, he was appointed *capitán a guerra* and protector of the Indians of San Diego del Mazapil. While holding this position, he is said to have rendered a great service in pacifying the Indians in the country surrounding Saltillo.[49] Here, as elsewhere, he is supposed to have done most of his work at his own expense, his own salary being only five hundred pesos in gold annually. While he was governor of Coahuila, from June 15, 1705, to January 30, 1708,[50] he succeeded in quieting the Indians of that region, part of whom he had to pacify by punishing severely the chiefs of their respective tribes.[51]

At the time of his appointment as leader of the new expedition into Texas, Alarcón was in Mexico City. On December 11, 1716, he advised the viceroy of the things that he would need for his journey[52] and at the same time requested that the total amount to be given him for the expedition be taken from the royal treasury of Guanajuato.[53] On December 22, 1716, he paid one hundred thirty-seven pesos as honorary fee for his appointment.[54]

Soon thereafter Alarcón must have left Mexico City to recruit his men for the expedition. While *en route* to Coahuila, he wrote the viceroy, on June 27, 1717, severely condemning the Ramón family and St. Denis (who had just returned to the Rio Grande) [55] for embarking on a gigantic commercial undertaking in which they planned to introduce French goods into Mexico. He recommended that St. Denis, then on his way to Mexico City, be kept prisoner in the capital, and enclosed letters from Olivares, who had preceded him to the Rio Grande, which also contained complaints against St. Denis and the Ramóns.[56] On August 3, 1717, Alarcón arrived at Monclova [57] and two days later took possession of the government of Coahuila.[58] He remained governor of Coahuila until November 16, 1719.[59]

Upon his arrival in Coahuila, Alarcón immediately investigated the affairs of St. Denis and his French henchmen in their trade with the Rio Grande settlements. The remaining Frenchmen took refuge in the mission of San Bernardo near the Rio Grande where Alarcón could not touch them, and in due time escaped into Texas. The missionaries and Captain Diego Ramón received Alarcón cordially, but from them he could obtain no information in regard to the activities of the Frenchmen. Father Muñoz, president of the Queretaran missions on the Rio Grande, knew nothing more than that the French goods had been brought in. In regard to the conditions at the presidio of San Juan Bautista he was more willing to give information. The soldiers there were not sufficient and those who were there were very neglectful of their duties. On August 17, 1717, after several more attempts had failed to get information from the inhabitants of the presidio and missions, Alarcón ordered Diego Ramón to deliver to him the fifteen mule-loads of goods that he had seized from St. Denis. When these were de-

CHURCH OF SAN JOSÉ Y SAN MIGUEL DE AGUAYO

livered, he made a vain attempt to get written statements
from persons at the presidio, but since they were all
friends of Ramón they had little to say.[60]

Alarcón, therefore, after placing the goods in the possession of Father Muñoz, turned his attention to the expedition. By September 18, 1717, he had recruited thirty-
five men, including six with families and a carpenter and
a mason.[61] Since he himself was to be delayed several
months more, toward the middle of November[62] he forwarded the supplies to the settlements in East Texas.[63]
At last, on March 11, 1718, final instructions were released for him,[64] which were based on the *dictámenes
fiscales* of November 30, 1716, and the decision of the
Junta General of December 2, 1716. According to these
instructions, Alarcón was to select fifty married soldiers,
preferably Spaniards, a carpenter, a mason, a blacksmith
and a weaver, and after he had assembled all his people
and his supplies on the Rio Grande, he was to proceed
immediately to the San Antonio river, traveling over the
most used roads, and keeping the people and herds in a
close group. He was to make moderate daily marches,
always keeping scouts in advance protected by at least
four soldiers, and employing enough Indian guides so as
not to travel over ground that had not been explored.
Every evening at the end of the day's march and each
morning before again starting out, he was to take a complete inventory of the expedition. To persons whom he
could trust, he was to delegate the duty of keeping
diaries, of which several were to be kept. In these were
to be noted the leagues traveled, the mountains, streams,
prairies and woodlands crossed, and the chief characteristics of each of these natural features of the land. From
time to time Alarcón was to send back reports of the
progress he had made. After arriving at the San Antonio
river, in accord with the missionaries, especially Father

Olivares, he was to found one or two missions between that river and the Guadalupe, helping the missionaries by giving them the necessary provisions, cattle, tools and the guard of ten soldiers granted to Olivares by the viceroy. With these supplies an Indian settlement was to be established, to which the Indians would be attracted by gifts from the missionaries. The Indians were to be pacified and converted by peaceful and affectionate means, preferably by treating with the Indian chiefs. Those who voluntarily became converted were, according to law, to be exempt for ten years from all involuntary tributes or services to the king. This did not, however, preclude their being persuaded to help the missionaries in the construction of the churches and other community work, for such coöperation would bring them more quickly into the art of civil living. In time two villas or cities were to be founded in the region near the San Antonio, Guadalupe and Colorado rivers, these cities to become the head and metropolis of the province and to serve as a protection against further foreign aggressions. Because of their location, these settlements would ultimately become the defense of all New Spain. In the meantime, a villa, to be founded near the missions on the San Antonio river, was to take their place. If the number of settlers for this villa did not reach thirty, Olivares was to be granted more than his ten soldiers for a guard. After founding the settlement on the San Antonio river, Alarcón was to proceed to the missions among the Texas Indians, leaving the soldiers designated for San Antonio under the command of the missionaries there. Once established, the soldiers at San Antonio were then with great diligence to explore the San Antonio, Guadalupe and Colorado rivers, making full reports on the origins, courses, fords, volumes of water and mouths of these streams, and the characteristics of the country through which they flowed.

Finally, before returning to Mexico from Texas, Alarcón
was to acquaint each official, lay and church, with these
instructions in order that they might know what duties
they were expected to perform.[65]

The expedition crossed the Rio Grande and got under
way on April 9, 1718. It consisted of seventy-two persons, including seven families, besides the cattle, sheep,
goats, chickens, six droves of mules, and 548 horses.
Alarcón traveled the route followed by previous expeditions until, on April 25th, he reached the San Antonio
river.[66] There, on May 1, 1718, he founded the mission
of San Antonio de Valero.[67] Four days later, three-fourths
of a league upstream from the mission, he founded the
Villa de Bejar,[68] and thus became the founder of modern
San Antonio, Texas. We must now return to Father
Olivares and follow his fortunes.

After receiving the viceroy's sanction for founding a
mission on the San Antonio river,[69] Father Olivares returned to Querétaro and prepared for his trip. He left
Querétaro on February 9, 1717, "with the companions
he had picked and all the provisions necessary for trans-
ferring the mission he expects to establish on the San Antonio river."[70] He arrived at the missions on the Rio
Grande on May 3d, and immediately asked the governor,
Don Joseph Antonio de Eca y Musquiz, for the two
soldiers he was to receive from the presidio of Coahuila,
and Captain Diego Ramón for the eight he was to be
given from the presidio of San Juan Bautista. Neither
official complied with his request, and Olivares, therefore, retired to the mission of San Joseph, four leagues
from the presidio of San Juan Bautista, to await the arrival of Alarcón. Alarcón arrived in Coahuila on August
3d, and Olivares remitted to him the viceregal orders, in
accordance with which Alarcón ordered the eight men
from the presidio of San Juan Bautista to be released and

placed under his orders, but not, as Olivares had wished, to be placed under Olivares' orders, so that they could take care of the supplies he stored away at San Joseph mission preparatory to leaving for the San Antonio river. For about eight more months they remained on the Rio Grande, and during this time, according to Olivares, more than 150 Indians, mostly chiefs, came to see him from the country near the San Antonio river. He told them of the plans he had of seeing them soon in their homeland and of the great desires that the king and the viceroy had for them to be converted and live in civil settlements. In order to prove to them that he was sincere, he showed them the many supplies that he had stored in the mission, and distributed some of the gifts among them, in return for which they promised to wait for him at the San Antonio river. Toward the middle of September, 1717, after he had noted that Alarcón had not recruited the fifty men he was to take on his expedition, Olivares wrote him asking for the ten soldiers designated for his use, in order that he could proceed to the San Antonio river. He indicated that if he were not given the soldiers soon, he would start out alone. But Alarcón took no heed of the letter and did not send him the soldiers until the following April. In the meantime, Olivares continued to write him, calling his attention to the desire of the viceroy that the soldiers they were to take along should be married and of good habits. To this Alarcón replied by asking Olivares where he was to get such people, since he had no "apostolical college" from which to take them and the people of Coahuila were of a very low order. Olivares finally left San Joseph mission on April 18, 1718, nine days after Alarcón had left the Rio Grande, and joined Alarcón in San Antonio on May 1st, the day on which Alarcón founded the mission of San Antonio de Valero. According to Olivares, whose

testimony may be discredited because of its contradictions, he received absolutely no aid from Alarcón; on the
contrary, Alarcón's behavior had kept the Indians from
coming to the mission.[71]

Having duly established the mission and villa on the
San Antonio river, Alarcón, in accordance with his instructions, set out immediately for the bay of Espíritu
Santo. He left Bejar on May 6th, and traveling over a
route roughly from San Antonio to present New Braunfels, thence to Seguin, and from there to Gonzales, he arrived at the junction of the Guadalupe and San Marcos
rivers. This perplexed him, since he thought the San
Marcos flowed into the Gulf. He, therefore, followed
the San Marcos upstream to its source near present San
Marcos, Texas, and from there returned to San Antonio.
On June 17th, he went back to the Rio Grande missions
for more supplies before he made any attempt to go to
East Texas. By August 27th he was back in San Antonio
where he received Father Espinosa and Captain Domingo
Ramón, who had come from East Texas to see about the
supplies destined for the missions among the Texas Indians. Together with these men, he left San Antonio for
the bay of Espíritu Santo and for East Texas on September 5th. After having made a thorough examination of
the bay region, he left it on September 24th and traveled
in a northeasterly direction over unexplored ground to
the missions among the Texas Indians. After many hardships, owing to the excessive rains, he arrived there on
October 14th. He stayed in East Texas until November
28th, visiting the missions, distributing gifts among the
Indians and receiving from them in turn many gifts and
demonstrations of loyalty, delivering supplies to the hard-
pressed soldiers and missionaries, and examining the
country for natural resources and for goods introduced
by the French. On the return trip he was detained for

twenty-two days on the flooded Trinity river, which he finally crossed under the greatest difficulty. It was not until January, 1719, that he again reached San Antonio.[72]

What became of Alarcón after founding the villa and mission at San Antonio and after his famous trip to the Texas missions, is still essentially a mystery. On April 27, 1719, he rendered to the viceroy a *consulta* in regard to a considerable amount of French merchandise that he had in his possession, and at the same time requested permission to come to Mexico City on official business. This request was denied him and he was ordered to send the goods to the nearest royal treasury.[73] Affidavits of the *cabildo* of the villa of Monclova, Coahuila, of September 22, 1719, of the *regimiento* of Nueva Tlaxcala, of December 2, 1719, and of the *comisario* of the Inquisition in Monclova, dated December 19, 1719, vouched for Alarcón's ability as governor during his term of office and lamented his departure, for since he had been in charge the province had experienced peace and prosperity. They testified to his great influence over the people whom he governed and praised his work in San Antonio.[74] Needless to say, these reports were exactly contrary to those of Olivares.[75]

For the services thus rendered to the king, Alarcón received royal thanks on October 31, 1719,[76] only two weeks before being relieved from office.[77] In November, 1721, he was in Mexico City, writing to the king complaining about the viceroy's treatment of him.[78] His last known act was to request the viceroy, in 1723, to give him news of a royal cedula which he had heard had been received and which redounded to his favor.[79]

With the finding of the diary of Alarcón's expedition and the testimonials attached to it, it is easier to obtain a more unbiased estimate of Alarcón's rôle in the early history of Texas. Probably owing to the fact that the

MAIN ENTRANCE AND A WINDOW OF THE CHURCH OF
SAN JOSÉ Y SAN MIGUEL DE AGUAYO

evaluation of his work has heretofore been based almost wholly on letters written by Father Olivares, the habitual complainer, and on letters written by the missionaries in East Texas before the arrival there of Alarcón, his efforts have been minimized.[80] With the discovery of the diary of his expedition, this estimate can now be changed to well-deserved praise. In addition, with the diary were found nine affidavits,[81] signed by missionaries and lay officials of East Texas, San Antonio and Coahuila, each of which is full of the highest praise for Alarcón, and can hardly be overlooked. Alarcón, perhaps, was rough and brutal when the occasion demanded. He may even have seen personally that the affidavits praising his work were duly written. He may have supervised the writing of the diary. Even so, it seems that he accomplished his task. Considering the fact that the year 1718 was one of excessive rains in Texas,[82] that Alarcón had a difficult time in recruiting the type of men he wished to take on his expedition, that Olivares offered little or no help and was in fact a constant hindrance, and that a great part of the country traversed by the expedition was unknown to the Spaniards until that day, one can but marvel at Alarcón's ultimate substantial accomplishments.

NOTES TO THE INTRODUCTION

1. The general historical outline presented in the following paragraphs is based on Charles Wilson Hackett, *Pichardo's Treatise on the Limits of Louisiana and Texas*, I, Austin, 1931; Hubert Howe Bancroft, *History of the North Mexican States and Texas*, I, San Francisco, 1884; Herbert Eugene Bolton and Thomas Maitland Marshall, *The Colonization of North America, 1492–1783*, New York, 1920; Herbert Eugene Bolton, *The Spanish Borderlands*, New Haven, 1921; William E. Dunn, *Spanish and French Rivalry in the Gulf Region of the United States, 1678–1702*, Austin, 1917; and Robert Carlton Clark, *The Beginnings of Texas, 1684–1718*, Austin, 1907.

2. El Colegio Apostólico de Propaganda Fide de la Santa Cruz de Querétaro, one of the autonomous houses of the Franciscan brotherhood, was founded in 1683. Besides Father Margil de Jesús, the college claimed such important figures of early American history as Father Espinosa and Fathers Francisco Garcés and Pedro Font, who made important explorations in California and Arizona. Herbert Eugene Bolton, *Guide to Materials for the History of the United States in the Principal Archives of Mexico*, p. 386, Washington, 1913.

3. It was also known as the presidio of San Juan Bautista del Rio del Norte. Near it was the mission of the same name, founded in 1699, and not far distant were the missions of San Bernardo, founded in 1703, and San Francisco Solano, founded by Father Olivares in 1700. It was this last mission and its Indians that were transferred to the San Antonio river by Olivares in 1718 to form the nucleus of the mission of San Antonio de Valero. The location of these missions was near present Guerrero, Coahuila, about thirty miles downstream from modern Eagle Pass, Texas. Fray Agustín Morfi, *Viage de Indios y Diario del Nuevo-México* in *Documentos para la Historia de México*, Tercera Serie, Tomo Primero, pp. 440–447, Mexico, 1856; Bancroft, *North Mexican States*, I, 607, note; Frederick Webb Hodge (ed.), *Handbook of American Indians North of Mexico*, II, 424, 437, Washington, 1910.

4. El Colegio Apostólico de Propaganda Fide de Nuestra Señora de Guadalupe de los Zacatecas was one of the autonomous houses of the Franciscan brotherhood. It was founded in Zacatecas in January, 1707, by Father Margil de Jesús and five other friars of the College of Santa Cruz de Querétaro. Isidro Felis de Espinosa, *El Peregrino Septentrional Atlante: Delineado en la Exemplarissima Vida del Venerable Padre F. Antonio Margil de Jesus*, pp. 231–242, Mexico, 1737; Fray Hermenegildo de Vilaplana, *Vida Portentosa del Americano Septentrional Apostol, el V. P. Fr. Antonio Margil de Jesus*, pp. 132–133, Madrid, 1775; Alberto Leduc and Luis Lara y Pardo, *Diccionario de Geografía, Historia y Biografía Mexicanas*, pp. 392, 589; Peter P. Forrestal, "The Venerable

Padre Fray Antonio Margil de Jesus," in *Preliminary Studies of the Texas Catholic Historical Society,* vol. II, No. 2 (April, 1932), pp. 18–19; and see also an interesting letter, written February 11, 1933, by the Reverend Luis de Palacio, of Zapopan, State of Jalisco, Mexico, to Señor Ing. Vito Alessio Robles, a copy of which is in the University of Texas Library, describing the organization of the Franciscan fathers in Mexico.

5. *El Gran Reyno de los Texas.* The Texas or Hasinai (Asinais) nation was a confederacy of the southern group of the Caddoan linguistic family of Indians. Their own name was *Hasínai,* meaning "our own folk." However, the Spaniards in coming in contact with the Hasinai heard the word *Texas, Texia,* or *Thecas* used by them to designate a large group of Caddoan and other tribes allied against the Apache, and attached to the Hasinai the name Texas, the word used by the Indians for "friends" or "allies." This was due mainly to the fact that the Hasinai were the first of the group of allies whom the Spaniards encountered and came to know intimately. Both Massanet and De León fell into the error of calling the Hasinai the Texas, but soon Francisco de Jesús María, a missionary left by Massanet among the Nabedache, a branch of the Hasinai group, wrote his report of August 15, 1691, in which he clarified the relationship among the Indians. He pointed out that the name *Texias,* or "friends," was a general name applied to a large group of tribes, about fifty in number, because of their long-standing friendship. Some of the tribes belonging to this group were not even a part of the Caddoan family. Terán, in 1691, dropped the name Texas and called the Indians by their real name, Asinai, the name applied by the Indians themselves to the group of tribes occupying the region around the Neches and Angelina rivers. Nevertheless, although Spanish residents in East Texas insisted that the correct name was Hasinai, the Spanish officials in New Spain continued to designate them as the *Texas* and their home as the "Province of the Texas." The most important tribes of the Neches-Angelina group of Indians were the Nabedache, Nacogdoche, Neche, Hainai, Nasoni, and Nadaco. Hodge, *Handbook,* I, 179–182; II, 738–741.

6. Herbert Eugene Bolton, "The Location of La Salle's Colony on the Gulf of Mexico," in *The Southwestern Historical Quarterly,* vol. XXVII, No. 3 (January, 1924), pp. 171–189.

7. Elizabeth Howard West, "De León's Expedition of 1689," in *The Quarterly* of the Texas State Historical Association, vol. VIII, No. 3 (January, 1905), pp. 199–224.

8. The Nabedaches were one of the Texas or Hasinai tribes living near the present Neches river.

9. The location of this mission has been definitely fixed at a point from one to two miles northwest of the present town of Weches, Houston County, Texas. Hodge, *Handbook,* II, 1–4, 436; Clark, *Beginnings of Texas,* pp. 24–25, 66; Eleanor Claire Buckley, "The Aguayo Expedition

into Texas and Louisiana, 1719–1722," in *The Quarterly* of the Texas State Historical Association, vol. XV, No. 1 (July, 1911), p. 43, note 2.

10. Clark, *Beginnings of Texas,* pp. 22–27, 33.

11. Most of the original documents relating to the Terán-Massanet expedition are to be found in the Archivo General de la Nación, Mexico City, *Provincias Internas,* vol. 182, ff. 220–317, 341–419, with manuscript copies of some of them in *Historia,* vol. 27, ff. 62–162; see also Mattie Austin Hatcher, "The Expedition of Don Domingo Terán de los Ríos into Texas," in *Preliminary Studies of the Texas Catholic Historical Society,* vol. II, No. 1 (January, 1932), and Clark, *Beginnings of Texas,* pp. 27–42.

12. Bancroft, *North Mexican States,* I, 404–405; Clark, *Beginnings of Texas,* p. 41; Bolton, *Spanish Borderlands,* p. 217.

13. The fort received its name from the Natchitoches Indians whom St. Denis settled at the place at the same time as a protection against Spanish encroachment and also as a base for opening commercial relations with the natives. Hodge, *Handbook,* II, 37.

14. Charmion Clair Shelby, "St. Denis's Second Expedition to the Rio Grande, 1716–1719," in *The Southwestern Historical Quarterly,* vol. XXVII, No. 3 (January, 1924), pp. 196–197.

15. Next to Margil, Espinosa was perhaps the most noted of the early missionaries in Texas. He is especially noted for his *Chrónica Apostólica y Seráphica de Todos los Colegios de Propaganda Fide de Esta Nueva-España,* published in Mexico in 1746. He had accompanied Father Olivares on a short expedition from the Rio Grande settlements into Texas in 1709.

16. Father Antonio Margil de Jesús, the outstanding missionary of early Texas history, was born in Valencia, Spain, in 1657. Coming to New Spain, he landed at Vera Cruz on June 6, 1683. He traveled over most of southern Mexico, and even into Central America. In 1687 he was *guardián* of the convent of Santa Cruz de Querétaro. He founded the Colegio del Cristo in Guatemala in 1701, and the Colegio de Nuestra Señora de Guadalupe de los Zacatecas in 1707. When the Ramón expedition left the Rio Grande, Margil was ill and could not accompany it. He left the Rio Grande on June 13th and arrived in East Texas soon after the missions had been established there by Espinosa for the College of Santa Cruz de Querétaro. For a more detailed life of Margil see Espinosa, *El Peregrino Septentrional;* Vilaplana, *Vida Portentosa;* and Forrestal, "Margil de Jesús."

17. The mission was reëstablished among the Nacoche Indians, at a place now identified as a few miles southwest of modern Alto, Cherokee County, Texas, near the Neche Indian mounds. Placed under the charge of the veteran missionary, Father Hidalgo, the mission was designed to serve the Nabedache, Neche, Nacachau (Nacoche), and Nacono tribes. Owing to an attack by the French from Louisiana, it was abandoned in

1719, to be reëstablished on August 5, 1721, by the Marqués de Aguayo and Father Espinosa. It was found without Indians by Rivera in 1727, and in 1730 it was finally withdrawn together with the missions of San José de los Nazones and Nuestra Señora de la Purísima Concepción. In 1731, after several attempts to place it on the San Marcos, Nueces, and Frio rivers, respectively, had been made, it was reëstablished on the San Antonio river and renamed San Francisco de la Espada. The remains of it may still be seen near San Antonio, but the buildings of the mission of San Francisco de los Texas must have been of wood, for no remains have been identified. Clark, *Beginnings of Texas,* pp. 66–67; Buckley, " Aguayo Expedition," pp. 45–46; Hodge, *Handbook,* II, 49–50, 435–436.

18. The location of the mission has been established at a point not far from modern Linwood crossing on the Angelina river. Before its removal tò San Antonio, the mission was sometimes called Nuestra Señora de la Purísima Concepción de los Aynais, Misión de la Purísima Concepción de los Asinays, and Misión de la Provincia de los Asinays. In 1719, with the other missions of East Texas, Purísima Concepción was abandoned owing to a French attack, and it was reëstablished by Aguayo and Fathers Espinosa and Margil in 1721. In 1731 it was removed to the San Antonio river together with the other two Queretaran missions, and was renamed Purísima Concepción de Acuña. Espinosa to Diez, February 28, 1718; Espinosa to the viceroy, February 28, 1718, MSS., A.G.N., *Provincias Internas,* vol. 181, ff. 130, 132–133; copies in *Historia,* vol. 27, ff. 270 (vuelta)–272, 272 (vuelta)–273, the copy of the letter to Diez being dated February 26 by mistake; Buckley, " Aguayo Expedition," pp. 46–47; Hodge, *Handbook,* II, 92–93; 329; Clark, *Beginnings of Texas,* p. 67.

19. The mission was founded among the Nazoni Indians on modern Bill's creek, one of the southern tributaries of Shawnee creek, near the northern boundary of present Nacogdoches county. Together with the other missions in East Texas, San Joseph was abandoned in 1719 because of a pending French attack. Father Espinosa and Aguayo refounded it on August 31, 1721, on the same site. In 1729–1730, with the abandonment of the presidio on the Angelina, the mission of San Joseph, together with those of Purísima Concepción and San Francisco de los Texas, was withdrawn. After attempts had been made to reëstablish it on the San Marcos river, then the Nueces and the Frio, it was finally reëstablished on the San Antonio river, seven miles below present San Antonio, and its name was changed to San Juan Capistrano, which name it bears today. *Representación hecha por el M.R. y Vener^e. P. Fr. Antonio Margil de Jesús,* February 13, 1718, MS. A.G.N., *Provincias Internas,* vol. 181, ff. 141–142; copies in *Historia,* vol. 394, ff. 168–169, and *Historia,* vol. 27, ff. 269–270; *Junta de Guerra y Hacienda,* December 2, 1716, MS., A.G.N., *Provincias Internas,* vol. 181, ff. 100, 103; *Historia,* vol. 27, ff. 262, 264; *Historia,* vol. 302, ff. 68, 70; *Historia,* vol. 394, ff. 149 (vuelta), 151 (vuelta) ; *Representación hecha por el Capitan Domingo Ramón a su Exª.,*

MS., A.G.N., *Historia,* vol. 27, ff. 205–208; Espinosa, *Diario Derrotero de la jornada a la Provincia de los Tejas,* July 30, 1716, MS., A.G.N., *Provincias Internas,* vol. 181, ff. 45–50, translation by Rev. Gabriel Tous in *Preliminary Studies of the Texas Catholic Historical Society,* vol. I, No. 4 (April, 1930); Ramon's Diary of the same expedition, MS., A.G.N., *Provincias Internas,* vol. 181, ff. 31–41; copy in *Historia,* vol. 27, ff. 181 (vuelta)–205, translated by Rev. Paul J. Foik in *Preliminary Studies of the Texas Catholic Historical Society,* vol. II, No. 5 (April, 1933); Hodge, *Handbook,* II, 442–443, 446; Buckley, "Aguayo Expedition," p. 48; and Clark, *Beginnings of Texas,* p. 67.

20. The mission was founded on the present site of Nacogdoches, Texas, among the Nacogdoche and Nacao Indians. The Nacogdoche were encountered by De Soto and his men, but they were made better known by the writings of Father Jesús María in 1691, who called them Nazadachotzi and classified them as one of the Aseney (Hasinai) tribes. Probably their closest allies and friends were the Nasoni. In 1719 the mission was abandoned together with the other missions of East Texas. It was reëstablished by Aguayo on the same location in 1721. Although it and the other Zacatecan missions were retained when the Queretaran missions were removed in 1730–1731, the mission of Nacogdoches never was successful. The Nacogdoche Indian village was moved soon thereafter to a site three leagues farther north, and in 1767 Rubí reported that the mission had not a single neophyte. With the cession of Louisiana to Spain in 1762, one of the main reasons for the mission's existence was removed, and in 1773 it was abandoned. In 1774 part of the settlers from Nacogdoches founded a settlement on the Trinity which they called Pilar de Bucareli, and five years later, without permission, they occupied some of the abandoned buildings of the former mission settlement of Nacogdoches, thus becoming the founders of the modern city of Nacogdoches, Texas. Hodge, *Handbook,* II, 6–8, 91; Buckley, *Aguayo Expedition,* pp. 48–49; Herbert Eugene Bolton, *Texas in the Middle Eighteenth Century,* pp. 375–446, Berkeley, 1915.

21. *Representación hecha por Margil de Jesús,* MS., A.G.N., *Provincias Internas,* vol. 181, ff. 141–142; *Historia,* vol. 27, ff. 269–270; *Historia,* vol. 394, ff. 168–169; *Junta de Guerra y Hacienda,* MS., A.G.N., *Provincias Internas,* vol. 181, f. 103; *Historia,* vol. 27, f. 264; *Historia,* vol. 302, f. 70; *Historia,* vol. 394, f. 151 (vuelta). The mistake made by Clark (*Beginnings of Texas,* p. 67) concerning the supervision of these missions was probably owing to the fact that three of the missions had names beginning with *Nuestra Señora.*

22. The mission was founded among the Eyeish (Ais, Ayish, Ayches, or Hais) Indians, and its site has been definitely fixed at modern San Augustine, Texas. It was abandoned with the other missions of East Texas in 1719, and was reëstablished by Aguayo in 1721, about a fourth of a league beyond the site that it had previously occupied. With the

cession of Louisiana to Spain in 1762 and the subsequent removal of the remaining missions in East Texas in 1773, the mission of Dolores de los Ais was definitely abandoned. The early home of the Eyeish, a tribe of the Caddo confederacy, was on Eyeish creek, between the Sabine and Neches rivers. The tribe was reported to have been little influenced by missionary activities in their midst, for after fifty years of effort only eleven baptisms were recorded at the mission. In 1768 Solís reported that they were licentious, thievish, drunken, and dangerous to the missionaries. *Representación por Margil de Jesús*, MS., A.G.N., *Provincias Internas*, vol. 181, ff. 141–142; *Historia*, vol. 27, ff. 269–270; *Historia*, vol. 394, ff. 168–169; Hodge, *Handbook*, I, 448–449, II, 94; Clark, *Beginnings of Texas*, p. 67; Buckley, "Aguayo Expedition," pp. 49–50; Espinosa, *El Peregrino Septentrional*, p. 280; and Vilaplana, *Vida Portentosa*, p. 155.

23. The mission was founded on January 29, 1717, about eight leagues west of Natchitoches, Louisiana. Together with the other missions in East Texas it was abandoned in 1719 owing to a pending French attack. It was reëstablished by Aguayo in 1721, about half a league beyond its previous location, or near the present town of Robeline, Louisiana. Across a stream from the mission, Aguayo established the presidio of Nuestra Señora del Pilar de los Adaes. This military post became the capital of the province of Texas, an honor it retained until 1773 when the remaining Spanish settlements in East Texas were abandoned. *Representación por Margil de Jesús*, A.G.N., *Provincias Internas*, vol. 181, ff. 141–142; *Historia*, vol. 27, ff. 269–270; *Historia*, vol. 394, ff. 168–169; Hodge, *Handbook*, II, 94, 450; Buckley, "Aguayo Expedition," pp. 50–52; Espinosa, *El Peregrino Septentrional*, p. 280; and Vilaplana, *Vida Portentosa*, p. 155.

24. It has been located as just west of the present town of Douglas, Nacogdoches county. It was abandoned with the missions in 1719, and reëstablished by Aguayo in 1721. In 1729 it was definitely abandoned. Hodge, *Handbook*, II, 92–93, 436; Buckley, "Aguayo Expedition," pp. 47, 48, 54.

25. After arriving in East Texas, St. Denis had continued on to Mobile, the French capital of Louisiana. There he immediately prepared for a second trip to the Rio Grande. By December, 1716, he was back among the Indians and missionaries of East Texas and aided the missionaries in many ways, providing food for them, helping them with the Indians over whom he had great influence, and aiding in the erection of their mission buildings. In March, 1717, he started out for the Rio Grande, accompanied by two other Frenchmen and by the Spanish *alférez* (ensign or standard bearer) of the Texas missions, whom Captain Domingo Ramón sent with dispatches to the governor of Coahuila. The expedition arrived at the presidio of San Juan Bautista on the Rio Grande in April, 1717, and there the goods were immediately seized by the captain in charge, Diego Ramón, father of Domingo Ramón and

grandfather of St. Denis by marriage. St. Denis was sent to Mexico City, where, after some delay, he was released on bond in November, 1717. He was allowed to return to the Rio Grande and to dispose of his goods. Having returned to Mexico City, he soon spent the money he had secured from the sale of his merchandise, and not receiving, as he had wished, a government position, he threatened to use his influence with the Indians to cause an uprising on the frontier. Threatened again with imprisonment because of these indiscretions, he was forced to flee from Mexico City, September 5, 1718. He arrived at Natchitoches on February 24, 1719, almost a month after Alarcón had received notice of his escape from Mexico City, as noted in the diary in the entry for January 29, 1719. See note 241 of the diary; Shelby, " St. Denis's Second Expedition," pp. 196–214; Clark, *Beginnings of Texas,* pp. 79–83.

26. Various letters and representations by Ramón and the missionaries in East Texas, MSS., A.G.N., *Provincias Internas,* vol. 181, ff. 30–31, 42–43, 51–52; *Historia,* vol. 27, ff. 177–182, 205–211; and Clark, *Beginnings of Texas,* pp. 70–71.

27. Diez to the viceroy, September 13, 1716, MS., A.G.N., *Provincias Internas,* vol. 181, f. 53; copies in *Historia,* vol. 27, f. 211; and *Historia,* vol. 394, f. 134; the copy in *Historia* gives by mistake the name of the writer as Joseph Diaz.

28. The first known missionary to go to the San Antonio river was Massanet. On Wednesday, June 13, 1691, he arrived at the San Antonio river and on the following day celebrated mass for the Indians he found there. His chapel consisted of a bower of twigs. The Indians there named the place *Yanaguana,* and for this Massanet substituted the Christian name of San Antonio de Padua in honor of St. Anthony of Padua. *Diario y Derrotero a la Provincia de los Tèchas,* MS., A.G.N., *Provincias Internas,* vol. 182, f. 305. The Ramón expedition reached the San Antonio on Thursday, May 14, 1716. They found a spring on level land, which they named San Pedro. They considered the place suitable for a city and recommended the spot for its " pleasantness, location, abundance of water, and multitude of fish." Tous, " Ramón Expedition: Espinosa's Diary of 1716," p. 9; Foik, " Captain Domingo Ramón's Diary of His Expedition into Texas in 1716," p. 12.

29. The Jarames or Xarames were a Coahuiltecan tribe, probably natives of the region around present San Antonio. They were in both the missions of San Juan Bautista and San Francisco Solano on the Rio Grande, being the chief tribe at the latter mission. A Jarame child was the first person baptized at the mission of San Antonio de Valero. Hodge, *Handbook,* II, 980.

30. The Payayas (Paia, Paiaia, Paillailles, Payaguas, or Payseyas) Indians were first known by Massanet who found them at the present site of San Antonio. It was for them that Massanet said mass in a chapel of twigs in 1691. (See note 28.) Some of the Payaya were baptized as

early as 1706 at the mission of San Francisco Solano. They are known to have ranged as far north as the Brazos river. Espinosa met them near the Brazos in 1716, and in 1717 Derbanne met them near the present Colorado. Rivera noted in 1727 that their most frequent home was on a creek bearing their tribal name, near the Medina river. Members of the tribe were inhabitants of the mission of San Antonio de Valero as late às 1776. Hodge, *Handbook,* II, 217–218, 425.

31. The Sana (Chanes, Zana, Canas or Chanas) Indians were probably a Tonkawan tribe. In 1691 Massanet met them beyond present Seguin, Texas. Ramón in 1716 mentioned the Chanas together with the Apaches and some other tribes as enemies of the Texas. Alarcón met some of the Xanac nation, probably the same tribe, just north of present Bellville. In 1721 Aguayo presented the Sanas in San Antonio with gifts, and later he met another part of the tribe near modern San Marcos. The Sana entered the mission of San Antonio de Valero from 1740 to 1749. Hodge, *Handbook,* II, 422–423; and the diàry, note 152.

32. The Pampoas (Pampopas or Pampapas) were a Coahuiltecan tribe living on the Nueces river as early as 1701. The usual abode was probably above the junction of the Frio and Nueces rivers, but Rivera in 1728 called them a roaming tribe. There were Pampoas in San Juan Bautista on the Rio Grande in the early eighteenth century. Although Father Olivares planned to place them in his mission of San Antonio de Valero, they entered rather the mission San José, founded a few years later, where they formed a part of the Indian population as late as 1793. Hodge, *Handbook,* II, 197.

33. Olivares to the viceroy, no date, dated by the fiscal November 20, 1716, MS., A.G.N., *Provincias Internas,* vol. 181, ff. 56–57; copies in *Historia,* vol. 27, ff. 215–216; *Historia,* vol. 394, ff. 134–140; *Memoria y Razón,* no date, *Provincias Internas,* vol. 181, ff. 120–121; and Espinosa, *Chrónica Apostólica,* p. 449.

34. Eusebio Gómez de la Puente (ed.), *Iconografía de Gobernantes de la Nueva España tomada de la colección que se conserva en el salón de cabildos del Palacio Municipal de la Cibdad de Mexico,* Mexico, 1921.

35. The shorter of the two is the *Dictamen del Fiscal,* signed by Dr. Espinosa, fiscal of the audiencia, and is to be found in A.G.N., *Provincias Internas,* vol. 181, ff. 57–59; copies in *Historia,* vol. 27, ff. 217 (vuelta)–221, *Historia,* vol. 302, ff. 31–34, and *Historia,* vol. 394, ff. 140–143. The other, more correctly known as *Resumen Arreglado,* is signed by Dr. Velasco, the *fiscal de hacienda,* and is to be found in *Provincias Internas,* vol. 181, ff. 60–89; copies in *Historia,* vol. 27, ff. 221–255, and vol. 302, ff. 35–61.

36. See the shorter of the *dictámenes,* the one signed by Dr. Espinosa. Cf. note 35 above.

37. See note 25, above, for the fortunes that awaited St. Denis on his second trip to the Rio Grande.

38. *Resumen Arreglado, Provincias Internas,* vol. 181, f. 78. From the beginning of Spanish occupancy of Texas, there was a great deal of confusion regarding which bay on the Texas coast was Espíritu Santo, all the bays surrounding modern Calhoun county being designated at one time or another as Espíritu Santo bay. Hackett, *Pichardo's Treatise,* I, 422, 423–459, 460.

39. Olivares to the viceroy, no date, dated by the fiscal November 20, 1716, MS., A.G.N., *Provincias Internas,* vol. 181, ff. 54–55.

40. Olivares to the viceroy, no date, *Provincias Internas,* vol. 181, ff. 56–57.

41. The Cadodachos (Kadohadachos, Caddo-dachos, Caddos or Cadogdachos) were one of the leading tribes of the Caddo confederacy, being often confused with the confederacy itself. Their first known contact with the white man occurred in 1541, when De Soto and his companions encountered some of the subtribes on the Washita river and near the Mississippi. In 1687 the survivors of La Salle's party visited them. Their relations with the French thereafter were always friendly. During the latter part of the eighteenth century they abandoned their habitat on the lakes of northwestern Louisiana and descended the Red river to settle not far from the Natchitoches Indians, their kindred. The name of the Caddos was extended by the whites to the confederacy of tribes belonging to the southern group of the Caddoan linguistic family. Their own name was *Hasínai.* (See note 5, above.) The southern group of the Caddos included such tribes as the Eyeish, Nacogdoches, Caddo-dachos, Nasoni, Natchitoches, and Adaes. Hodge, *Handbook,* I, 179–182, 638–639.

42. See the *Resumen Arreglado,* mentioned in note 35, above.

43. *Ibid., Provincias Internas,* vol. 181, ff. 81 (vuelta)–82.

44. *Junta General,* December 2, 1716, MS., A.G.N., *Provincias Internas,* vol. 181, ff. 91–110; copies in *Historia,* vol. 27, ff. 255–269; *Historia,* vol. 302, ff. 62–73; and *Historia,* vol. 394, ff. 143–145. The copy in *Historia,* vol. 27, is known as *Junta de Guerra y Hacienda.*

45. Decree of the viceroy, December 7, 1716, MS., A.G.N., *Provincias Internas,* vol. 181, ff. 111–112, with a copy in *Historia,* vol. 394, ff. 156–157. This decree was only in the form of an *acuerdo* or order to draw up the papers which the viceroy signed two days later, December 9th, the date usually given for the appointment of Alarcón. Decree of the viceroy, December 9, 1716, MS., A.G.N., *Provincias Internas,* vol. 183, ff. 154–159; Bolton, *Guide,* p. 478; *Relación de los Empleos Méritos y Servicios del Sargento Mayor Don Martín de Alarcón,* January 18, 1721, MS., A.G.N., *Historia,* vol. 27, f. 289; *Historia,* vol. 394, f. 233. Both of the manuscript copies of the *Relación* are copies of an original that has not been found. The copy in *Historia,* vol. 27, gives the date of Alarcón's appointment as February 9th, but this is an error, an error which Bancroft made subsequently when he used the same document. *North Mexican States,* I, 614. The *Relación* also states that Alarcón was named governor

of Texas while holding the office of governor of the presidio de Coahuila, but no other documents have been found giving information as to when he was appointed to the latter office which he took charge of on August 5, 1717. The king's approval of the action taken by the viceroy was given on June 11, 1718. Royal cedula, June 11, 1718, MS., A.G.N., *Historia,* vol. 298, ff. 148 (vuelta)–151; *Historia,* vol. 321, ff. 57–60; Juan Agustín Morfi, *Historia de la Provincia de Texas,* MS., Archivo del Convento Grande de San Francisco in the Biblioteca Nacional in Mexico City, Legajo 100, ff. 40–41; a translation of this document has been made by Dr. Carlos E. Castañeda, entitled *Morfi's History of Texas,* MS., Doctor's Dissertation, University of Texas Library, Austin, 1932; and Elizabeth Howard West, "Bonilla's Brief Compendium of the History of Texas, 1772," in *The Quarterly* of the Texas State Historical Association, vol. VIII, No. 1 (July, 1904), p. 30.

46. Decree of the viceroy, December 7, 1716, MS., A.G.N., *Provincias Internas,* vol. 181, f. 113; copy in *Historia,* vol. 394, f. 157. It is interesting to note that the idea of the viceroy was to place the mission on the San Antonio river about twenty or twenty-five leagues from the bay of Espíritu Santo, but the settlement was finally placed about fifty leagues from the bay.

47. The document is the *Relación* cited in note 45, above.

48. For a discussion of the militia (*milicias*) in New Spain, see Agustín Rivera, *Principios Críticos sobre el Vireinato de la Nueva España,* p. 82, San Juan de los Lagos, 1884.

49. According to the *Relación* he brought more than a thousand families of Indians together and settled them in a town which he named San Esteban. If this statement intends to give credit to Alarcón for the founding of San Esteban de Nueva Tlaxcala, an Indian settlement which in those days was near Saltillo and today is a part of it, it is untrue, for San Esteban was founded in 1591 by Francisco de Urdiñola. Vito Alessio Robles, *Francisco de Urdiñola y el Norte de la Nueva España,* pp. 169–190. Alarcón was cognizant of the fact that the Indian settlement had the name of San Esteban de Nueva Tlaxcala, for on March 29, 1699, a document was signed before him as protector of the Indians in which that name was used. *Autos fechos de pedimento de los Naturales del Pueblo de San Esteban de la Nueva Tlaxcala, de Santiago del Saltillo, de la Jurizdiccion de la Nueva Viscaya; en que se quejan de las vejaciones molestias y agravios que resiven de los españoles de la Villa del Saltillo,* MS., A.G.N., *Tierras,* vol. 168, segunda parte, ff. 1–17.

50. Documents furnished by Señor Cosme Garza García, for many years *Oficial Mayor* of the government of the state of Coahuila, copies of which are in the possession of Señor Ing. Vito Alessio Robles.

51. *Relación, Historia,* vol. 27, ff. 287–288; *Historia,* vol. 394, ff. 231–232.

52. Alarcón to the viceroy, December 11, 1716, MS., A.G.N., *Provincias Internas,* vol. 181, f. 115; copy in *Historia,* vol. 394, f. 158.

53. The total amount granted him, to be paid one year in advance, beginning January 1, 1718, was 28,150 pesos. This included his salary for one year, of 2,500 pesos, the salaries of fifty soldiers at 400 pesos each, the salary of an engineer at 450 pesos, the salaries of a mason, a carpenter, and a blacksmith at 400 pesos each, and 4,000 pesos for supplies to be taken to the missions in East Texas. Alarcón to the viceroy, no date, dated by the viceroy December 11, 1716, MS., A.G.N., *Provincias Internas,* vol. 181, ff. 117–118; copy in *Historia,* vol. 394, ff. 159–160.

54. Certificate of Juan del Olmo, MS., A.G.N., *Provincias Internas,* vol. 181, f. 119; copy in *Historia,* vol. 394, ff. 160 (vuelta)–161.

55. See note 25, above.

56. Shelby, " St. Denis's Second Expedition," pp. 202–203.

57. *Ibid.,* p. 204; Olivares to the viceroy, June 22, 1718, MS., A.G.N., *Provincias Internas,* vol. 181, ff. 147–153; copy, incomplete, in *Historia,* vol. 394, ff. 172–177.

58. *Certificación del cabildo de Santiago de Monclova,* August 6, 1717, MS., A.G.N., *Provincias Internas,* vol. 181, f. 127; *Relación, Historia,* vol. 27, f. 292, and vol. 394, f. 236.

59. Documents furnished by Garza García. The *Relación* says that he was still governor on December 19, 1719. *Historia,* vol. 27, f. 291 (vuelta) and vol. 394, f. 236.

60. Shelby, " St. Denis's Second Expedition," pp. 204–208.

61. *Certificación del cabildo de Santiago de Monclova,* September 18, 1717, MS., A.G.N., *Provincias Internas,* vol. 181, ff. 128–129. This document gives a list of the persons whom Alarcón had recruited, which differs very little from the list presented by Olivares in June, 1718, after the settlement on the San Antonio had been made. Olivares to the viceroy, June 22, 1718, *Provincias Internas,* vol. 181, f. 153.

62. *Testimonio del título de Governador y Instrucciones que se le dió a Don Martín de Alarcón p^a. la entrada que hizo en la Provincia de los Tejas,* MS., A.G.N., *Provincias Internas,* vol. 183, f. 162; *Historia,* vol. 394, f. 212 (vuelta) ; and *Historia,* vol. 27, f. 275.

63. Alarcón sent the supplies with Father Miguel Núñez de Aro and four soldiers. On January 28, 1718, the party arrived at a lake called Santa Ana, about fourteen leagues west of the Trinity and forty-eight leagues from the East Texas settlements, and there they stayed for more than two months blocked by floods. During this time they subsisted on some roots and a little corn given them by Indians. Finally, driven by hunger and seeing no other way out of their predicament, on March 30th they turned back after having first hidden the supplies in a wood and covered them with the missionary's tent and having written letters to Captain Ramón in East Texas, which they left with some Texas

Indians to be delivered as soon as the floods subsided. On their return
trip, April 21st, they encountered the Alarcón expedition just southwest
of the Medina river. Alarcón heard Núñez' tale and accordingly soon
sent out two successive expeditions to recover the supplies, but both of
them failed. On June 17, 1718, Alarcón returned to the Rio Grande for
additional supplies before going to East Texas. In the meantime letters
had arrived from the missionaries in East Texas telling of their great
need for help, and, therefore, from the Rio Grande Alarcón sent a third
expedition to recover the supplies. This expedition left the Rio Grande
on June 27, 1718, and consisted of Father Pedro Muñoz, president of the
Rio Grande missions, Father Núñez, an *alférez*, and nine soldiers. In
case they should not find the hidden cargoes, Alarcón sent along additional supplies and gifts for the Indians, which they were to take to
East Texas. This small expedition arrived at Santa Ana lake on July 21,
and soon found the supplies just as Núñez had left them. In the meantime Captain Domingo Ramón in East Texas had on June 20, 1718, received the letters left by Núñez with the Texas Indians, and accordingly
set out with Fathers Espinosa and Mathías Saenz de San Antonio to recover the hidden supplies. They met Father Muñoz at the lake four days
after the latter had arrived there, and the two parties returned together
to San Antonio where they arrived on August 27. When, on September
5th, Alarcón left San Antonio for Espíritu Santo bay and the East Texas
settlements, all of these people accompanied him except Father Saenz who
continued to Mexico to plead with the viceroy for more assistance. Before
Saenz arrived in Mexico City, however, the letters from the missionaries
in East Texas had been forwarded from the Rio Grande, and on June
27, 1718, the viceroy discussed before a *junta de hacienda* the problem
of aiding the missionaries. Not knowing of the efforts that Alarcón was
making to recover the supplies hidden by Núñez, and considering them
lost, the junta appropriated another 4,000 pesos for the relief of the
missionaries. Saenz arrived in Mexico City in November and presented
to the viceroy the hardships of the missionaries and the great risk Spain
was running of losing the settlements to the French who had a fort on
the Red river and were building many more along the Mississippi. But,
owing to the great delay, Saenz grew tired of waiting for additional
aid, and in February, 1719, left the capital with only the amount previously appropriated. *Certificación de Francisco de Céliz,* August 31, 1718,
MS., A.G.N., *Tierras,* vol. 360; *Certificación de Domingo Ramón,* September 1, 1718, MS., *ibid.;* Margil de Jesús to the viceroy, February 13,
1718, MS., A.G.N., *Provincias Internas,* vol. 181, ff. 141–142; copies in
Historia, vol. 27, ff. 269–270; vol. 394, ff. 168–169; Espinosa to the viceroy, February 28, 1718, MS., A.G.N., *Provincias Internas,* vol. 181, f. 130
(vuelta); copy in *Historia,* vol. 27, ff. 272 (vuelta)–273; Espinosa to
Diez, February 28, 1718, MS., A.G.N., *Provincias Internas,* vol. 181, ff.
132–133; copy in *Historia,* vol. 27, ff. 270 (vuelta)–272; Hidalgo to

Diez, March 11, 1718, MS., A.G.N., *Provincias Internas,* vol. 181, f. 146;
Hidalgo to the viceroy, April 18, 1718, MS., A.G.N., *Provincias Internas,*
vol. 181, f. 134; copy in *Historia,* vol. 27, ff. 273 (vuelta)–274; Diego
Ramón to the viceroy, May 30, 1718, MS., A.G.N., *Provincias Internas,*
vol. 181, f. 139; Diez to the viceroy, June 16, 1718, MS., A.G.N., *Pro-
vincias Internas,* vol. 181, f. 140; *Junta de Hacienda,* June 27, 1718, MS.,
ibid., ff. 143–145; Espinosa, *Chrónica Apostólica,* pp. 444–446, 450–451.
Espinosa (*Chrónica Apostólica,* p. 450) gives Saenz's name as Sans, and
Domingo Ramón in his diary of 1716 gave his name as Sanches (Foik,
"Ramón's Diary," p. 8), but an original signature gives his name as
Saenz. *Certificación de los R.R.P.P. Misioneros,* no date, MS., A.G.N.,
Provincias Internas, vol. 181, f. 43 (vuelta); copy in *Historia,* vol. 27, f.
208.

64. These were perhaps the same instructions that Alarcón received
soon after he had begun his march. See diary, entry for April 16th. The
information contained in the diary indicates that the instructions were
carried out almost to the letter.

65. *Testimonio del título de Governador y Instrucciones que se le dió
a Don Martín de Alarcón, Provincias Internas,* vol. 183, ff. 160–173;
Espinosa, *Chrónica Apostólica,* pp. 447–449.

66. See diary, p. 48.

67. Missionaries at San Antonio to Francisco Xavier Ortiz, March 6,
1762, MS., A.G.N., *Historia,* vol. 28, f. 164; another copy is in the Archivo
del Convento Grande de San Francisco, B.N., legajo 99, no. 3. Father
Olivares arrived at San Antonio on May 1, but it is not known whether
he appeared in time for the founding of his mission. Olivares to the
viceroy, June 22, 1718, *Provincias Internas,* vol. 181, ff. 147–152. These
facts disprove the statement made by Castañeda and quoted by Chabot,
that the mission of San Antonio de Valero was established *de facto* long
before 1718. Castañeda and Chabot based their statement on this letter
of Olivares, the one from Diez to the viceroy cited in note 70, the letters
from Olivares to the viceroy cited in notes 33 and 39, and on the *junta
general* cited in note 44, but they did not have the diary with which to
supplement this information. Castañeda, *Morfi's History of Texas,* MS.,
pp. 216–217, note 23; Frederick C. Chabot, *Excerpts from the Memorias
for the History of the Province of Texas,* p. xvi, notes 30 and 33; p.
59, note 6, San Antonio, 1932. The statement made by Espinosa (*Chrónica
Apostólica,* p. 449) that Olivares founded the mission of San Antonio de
Valero some time before Alarcón reached the San Antonio river, may
also now be rejected. The mission was named in honor of San Antonio
de Padua (see note 28, above), and of the viceroy, Baltasar de Zúñiga,
Guzmán Sotomayor y Mendoza, Marqués de Valero.

68. The settlement was probably named in honor of either the town
or district by that name in the province of Salamanca, Spain. The *Relación* gives the settlement also the name of San Antonio de los Llanos.

Historia, vol. 27, ff. 289 (vuelta), 291 (vuelta); *Historia,* vol. 394, ff. 234, 235 (vuelta). The first census of San Antonio, taken June 14, 1718, or only six weeks after its founding, gives the following military company at San Antonio: Governor Don Martín de Alarcón, Military engineer Don Francisco Barreiro y de Álvarez, Captain Santiago Ximénez, Alférez Francisco Hernández, Sergeant Juan Barrera, and the following soldiers: Cristóbal de Carvajal, Vicente Guerra, Sebastián González, Joseph de Neyra, Joseph Velásquez, Joseph Ximénez, Antonio Guerra, Gerónimo Carvajal, Juan Domingo, Joseph Chirino, Juan Valdés, Francisco Rodríguez, Matheo Rodríguez, Francisco Menchaca, Joseph Antonio Rodríguez, Marcelino Zicona, Nicolas Hernández, Francisco Hernández, Andrés de Sosa, Juan de Castro, Domingo Flores, Joseph Maldonado, Manuel Maldonado, Juan Galván, Patricio de la Cruz, Joseph Placido Flores, Antonio Pérez, Agustín Pérez, Joseph Cadena, Cristóbal de la Garza, Miguel Hernández, and Juan de Sosa. Olivares to the viceroy, June 22, 1718, *Provincias Internas,* vol. 181, f. 152.

69. See p. 18.

70. Diez to the viceroy, February 10, 1717, MS., A.G.N., *Provincias Internas,* vol. 181, f. 126.

71. Olivares to the viceroy, June 22, 1718, *Provincias Internas,* vol. 181, ff. 147–152; copy in *Historia,* vol. 394, ff. 172–177. This letter was written mainly to discredit Alarcón and is full of contradictions and complaints.

72. This paragraph is based on the diary.

73. *Otro [mandamiento] del virrey,* July 31, 1719, MS., A.G.N., *Historia,* vol. 394, ff. 222 (vuelta)–223. Morfi says that as soon as Alarcón had founded San Antonio he asked the viceroy for additional money and equipment and another 175 soldiers, and that this request being denied him, he became angry and resigned. It is not known on what documents Morfi based this statement. *Historia de la Provincia de Texas,* Archivo del Convento Grande de San Francisco, B.N., legajo 100, no. 15, ff. 40–41. See also Bancroft, *North Mexican States,* I, 614.

74. *Relación, Historia,* vol. 27, ff. 289–293; *Historia,* vol. 394, ff. 233 (vuelta)–237.

75. See note 71, above.

76. *Relación, Historia,* vol. 27, ff. 293 (vuelta)–294; *Historia,* vol. 394, ff. 237–238.

77. He was relieved from office on November 16, 1719, but was still performing the same duties on December 19, 1719. Documents furnished by Cosme Garza García; *Relación, ibid.,* vol. 394, f. 236.

78. Alarcón to the king, November 3, 1721, MS., A.G.N., *Historia,* vol. 394, ff. 238 (vuelta)–241.

79. Alarcón to the viceroy, no date, dated by the viceroy April 17, 1723, and by the *fiscal* on April 22, 1723, MS., A.G.N., *Historia,* vol. 394, ff. 241 (vuelta)–242.

80. See Morfi, *Historia de la Provincia de Texas,* Archivo del Convento Grande de San Francisco, B.N., legajo 100, no. 15, ff. 40–41; West, "Bonilla's Brief Compendium," pp. 30–31; Bancroft, *North Mexican States,* I, 614–615; and Hackett, *Pichardo's Treatise,* I, 225.

81. MSS., A.G.N., *Tierras,* vol. 360.

82. The accounts in the diary concerning the swollen streams give sufficient proof of this. Captain Domingo Ramón states that he had never experienced a season of rains like that of 1718. *Certificación de Domingo Ramón,* September 1, 1718, *Tierras,* vol. 360.

DIARY OF THE ALARCÓN EXPEDITION INTO TEXAS, 1718–1719

HERE begins the diary of the expedition which was made to the Bay of Spiritu [*sic*] Santo and the Province of the Tejas by General Don Martín de Alarcón, Knight of the Order of Santiago, Governor and Lieutenant Captain-General of the Provinces of Coahuila, New Kingdom of the Philippines,[1] Province of the Tejas.

Today, April 9th, of the year 1718, the expedition crossed the Rio Grande del Norte.[2] It consists of seventy-two persons, including the muleteers, and seven families. The cattle, sheep, chickens, six droves of mules laden with clothing and provisions, and five hundred and forty-eight horses were also crossed from the other side of the aforesaid river on this day.

This same day, the governor left the mission of San Juan Baptista del Rio del Norte, and the camp[3] left the aforementioned place and stopped at Las Rosas de San Juan.[4] This road, after leaving the river and to the Real del Cuerbo,[5] is rough, craggy, and mountainous, owing to the hills near the river. The rest of the road is even, and although at present it is pleasing because of the verdure owing to the rains, the greater part of the time, the residents say, these fields are not so pretty, because the water which the river carries to the said place exists only when it rains. It is about seven leagues[6] from the mission of San Juan Baptista, and, as I say, water is not always to be had.

On the 10th, we left the above-mentioned spot,[7] and went to that of El Carrizo,[8] which is about seven leagues distant. This road is level for the first three leagues; the rest is hilly in places and with some ravines. There is a spring at this place, which is very lovely, owing to the willows extending up the creek, although the water itself is not sufficient for tillage.[9]

On the 11th of the said month, the camp did not leave this place, because the day before one of the herds was left on the road; on the 12th, having gathered the herds, the camp left the above-named place[10] for the creek of Caramanchel,[11] which is about three leagues distant. The road is open because, although there is woodland, it is clear. In this creek there is no water at the crossing except when it rains, and then it is bad because of the silt.

On the 13th, the camp did not leave this spot because it was raining early in the morning. On this day an Indian of the Pacuaxin nation,[12] who was roaming near the camp hunting for game for food, was brought in, and after the governor had spoken to him, he made him gifts and ordered him to take the Indian guide and a soldier to his settlement, so that some Indians of his nation could return with them, for he wanted to give them presents.

On the 14th, before leaving the above-mentioned place,[13] the soldier and the Indian guide arrived with nine Indians of the said nation, whom the governor regaled with tobacco and flour. This same day, the camp left the above-said place and went to that of Los Charcos de los Encinos,[14] which is about three leagues distant. The road is smooth and little wooded. After two and a half leagues there is a creek of running water which those who have seen it before say is from a freshet owing to the rains above it. This site is a very deep creek, overgrown with oaks and some elms, and contains water when it rains.

On the 15th, the camp left the said place for El Charco de Ranas,[15] which is about four leagues distant. The road is all level ground. About a league after having started we passed the river which they call *de las Nuezes*.[16] Its bed is very deep and is bordered by oaks, pecans,[17] elms, and some mulberry trees. This river does not have permanent water at the crossing. El Charco de Ranas contains rainwater, and there are many elms, oaks, live oaks, and some pecans.

On the 16th, the expedition left the above-mentioned camp [18] for that of La Resureccion [19] which is about six leagues distant. The governor gave it this name because we had arrived there on Holy Saturday. This creek is somewhat deep in places and in several pools has very turbid, bad-smelling, and stagnant rainwater. It is bordered by some oaks and St. John's roses. The road is smooth all the way and with some flowers, it being the time for them. There is also much wild red marjoram and hemp hay. While here, two Indians of the Pacuaxin nation arrived, whom the governor received kindly and presented with tobacco. During the afternoon two soldiers also arrived at this place, one from the presidio of Coahuila, and the other from that of Rio del Norte. They brought a dispatch from the most excellent viceroy [20] for the governor, giving him the orders he is to execute. According to these, being required to go straight to Tejas, the said governor had to go first to the bay of Spiritu Santo, in conformity with the desire of his Excellency.

On the 17th, the camp left the above-mentioned place [21] for that of La Hedionda.[22] The governor gave it this name, because of its not having had it before, and because it is a ravine containing little water, and this muddy and ill-tasting and ill-smelling. About two and a half leagues from this spot a dry creek was crossed, then a hill covered with flint, and then the Frio river,[23] which is also dry. Both rivers and creeks are densely bordered by

very tall oaks and thick woods. There are also grapes
with the fruit as large as a good-sized rifle-ball, but the
inside of the grape which is found here and henceforward
in many places, changes upon ripening into a wool-like
substance. The rest of the road is level and overgrown
with grass. Here many deer and turkeys thrive. Eight
leagues were traveled today.[24]

On the 18th, the expedition left the said place and
traveled to the Arroyo Hondo,[25] which is about two and
a half leagues distant, a league and a half of level ground
and without woodland and the other league of forests, in
places very thick, although the road is open. Before
reaching the above-named creek one crosses another
which is very deep.[26] At the crossing there is a giant
pecan, and for a distance on both sides stand many other
pecans and oaks. In the creek at this place there is water,
although it is very muddy owing to the fact that it comes
from the rains. They say that ordinarily it is dry. At its
outlet this creek forms a ravine which runs straight for
about a quarter of a mile [27] before coming out on the
plain. This creek and its surroundings are very overgrown
with oaks, pecans, poplars, and elms.

On the 19th, the camp left this place [28] for that of El
Tulillo,[29] which is about four and a half leagues distant;
a league and a half is wooded, but the wood is open and
unencumbered so that one may easily gallop on horseback. About another league farther on there is a hill, not
very high, and aside from this, the rest of the way is
level. This place of El Tulillo is delightful because of the
many and different flowers with which it is covered. There
is water on the plain. It is not a stream, but rainwater.

On the 20th, the camp left the above-said site and
traveled toward Los Charcos de la Pita,[30] which is about
three leagues distant. This road for the greater part is
level and is wooded in only a few places. These pools

are bordered by oaks, on which some tangled grapevines grow. Those who have passed here at other times say that a vein of metal runs along the center of the ravine, but at present it was not found because the ravine was full of water owing to the excessive rains. This pool supplies itself from rainwater.

On the 21st, the camp left this pool for the creek of Los Payayas,[31] which is about three leagues distant. All this road is densely bordered by mesquites, oaks, and pecans. Half-way on this day's march we were met by the father preacher Fray Miguel Núñez,[32] resident of the College of Nuestra Señora de Guadalupe de los Zacatecas.[33] He is the one who, during the month of December, started with the relief for the reverend fathers of the province of the Tejas. He said that on the 28th of January they had arrived at a lake [34] which is about fourteen leagues distant from the Trinity river, and not being able to go on, owing to the great floods of the rivers, he was detained there in company with four soldiers until the 30th of March. During this time they lived for the first few days on some corn which the Tejas Indians, who were living there, gave them. The remaining days [they subsisted] on roots of the field which other Indians gave them, and the latter having left, because the time was arriving for planting their crops, and the said father and soldiers seeing themselves suffering from hunger and without hope of being able to take the cargo to Tejas nor being able to send a notice to the said fathers because no Indians dared to cross [the river] by swimming, they decided to return, leaving the cargo hidden in a wood, protected by the tent which the said father carried along for his shelter. They stated that when, on their return, they came to two creeks and the Colorado river,[35] since they had not brought back the cargo, they all crossed by swimming. The father arrived sick, pale, and thin, [and said

that he had] left letters with a Tejas Indian to be taken
to the fathers when the rivers subsided. In these he told
them what had happened and gave them directions as to
where the place was where the supplies were left.

On the 22d, the camp did not leave the said place,[36] because it had rained a great deal the afternoon preceding.
On the 23d, it left for the Medina river,[37] which is about
six leagues distant. The road is level, without hills or
ravines, but with many groves of trees. The way is bordered by different herbs and many different flowers.

On the 24th, we crossed the Medina river with some
difficulty because it had rained and the river was running.
This river is densely shaded by poplars, elms, mulberries,
savins,[38] and hackberries.

On the 25th, the camp left this place for the San Antonio river, which is about six leagues distant.[39] The road
is mountainous to the cañon which they call De León,[40]
which is about three leagues from the above-named place.
The remainder of the road is level. In this place of San
Antonio there is a spring of water which is about three-
fourths of a league from the principal river.[41] In this lo-
cality, in the very spot on which the villa of Bejar was
founded,[42] it is easy to secure water, but nowhere else.
At the upper end of the said spring is a thick wood of
different trees, such as elms, poplars, hackberries, oaks,
and many mulberries and brambleberries, and the rest of
the wood is covered with grapevines from the ground up.
On this day two squads left the camp to examine the river
above and below. In the upper part, which is where the
governor went, nothing of use could be found, because
those who understand the matter say that a place to draw
water may be had only with much difficulty and expense;
the captain who went to the lower end, to where the first
creek joins the river, says that there is no place whatsoever to draw water, because the river flows in a very deep

channel. They did not go any farther since it had begun
to rain.

On the 5th of May,[43] the governor, in the name of his
Majesty, took possession of the place called San Antonio,
establishing himself in it, and fixing the royal standard
with the requisite solemnity, the father chaplain having
previously celebrated mass, and it was given the name of
villa de Bejar. This site is henceforth destined for the
civil settlement and the soldiers who are to guard it, as
well as for the site of the mission of San Antonio de
Valero,[44] established by the said governor about three-
fourths of a league down the creek.

On the 6th of the said month, the governor, with
twenty-five men and the father chaplain, left in search of
the bay of Spiritu Santo and arrived at the creek which
they call Síbulo,[45] which is about eight leagues from the
above-named place. On the way, at three leagues' distance, a creek which they call Salado[46] is encountered. It
is bordered by trees such as live oaks, hackberries, and
elms. There are also brambleberries and wild herbs on
the banks. On the remainder of the way several ravines
are found, all of them dry. All of the land is rough and
overgrown with mesquites and very tall bushes so that
one can hardly see the men on horseback.

On the 7th, the governor left the said place for the
second river of Guadalupe,[47] which is about seven leagues
away. At five leagues a creek was found with little water,
which, since it did not have a name, the governor called
Arroyo de San Miguel.[48] Afterwards, at about half a
league, one encounters the river of Guadalupe, the first
branch,[49] and from this to the second [branch][50] the distance is about a league and a half. The creek as well as
the two rivers are densely overgrown with poplars, oaks,
savins, and pecans, and many mulberries and grapevines.
So far as can be noticed, water cannot be extracted here

owing to the great depth that it has.[51] The governor reconnoitered to the junction of the two branches[52] of this river, which is about two leagues from the ford,[53] and his Lordship says that its flow is as great as that of La Veracruz Vieja.[54]

On the 8th of the said month, mass having been celebrated, the governor, in the name of his Majesty, took possession of the two rivers of Guadalupe, fixing the royal standard on the said location as an indication of possession. The said place was left at about eight o'clock that day for the creek of Salsipuedes,[55] to which the governor gave that name because it is located in a thick wood. It is about ten leagues from the river of Guadalupe. The road is about four leagues of good and open ground; the rest of woods. This day we traveled between east and southeast, and many detours were made to avoid the thick woods, the compass being used because the two Indian guides had fled fearful of the other Indians who live on the coast.

On the 9th, the said place was left for a creek which the governor named Entraaverlo,[56] because near it are two other creeks, very deep and miry, and the wood is thick, so that in order to extricate oneself from this entanglement of very high trees, grapevines, and *cocolmecates*,[57] one calls loudly for a knife. The rest of the way is wooded, but passable. It is about ten leagues from one place to the other. All the way is rough and full of dry creeks. At seven leagues we came across the river of San Marcos,[58] which runs very deep. There are rocks in various places. All the bank could not be reconnoitered owing to the density of the forest. Bison roam on this land, a fact known by the many tracks that are seen.

On the 10th, a place[59] was reached where the company was baffled as to whether to follow a river which we judged to be the San Marcos. At a distance of about four and a half leagues from the above-named place, this river joins the Guadalupe river, which is deep and swift, and for this reason it was recognized that the other was not the real San Marcos river.[60] In this spot it forms a pasture ground, large and suitable for raising cattle, and since we had lost ourselves, we retraced our steps about a league and half in order to go in search of the origin of this river and to inspect its source. It is densely overgrown with live oaks, oaks, poplars, and pecans, and other trees that are unidentified. Near the junction of the said rivers there are also many buckthorn trees. As soon as we stopped in the said pasture, the governor went upstream to see if he could find a ford, and on the way his Lordship saw two Indians who, with loads on their backs, were walking toward the woods. They were called, but, not recognizing the people, they took flight. This day we traveled south [61] in order to follow the bank of the river. Some crosses were left on the trees for the Indians as a sign, and on them some leaves of tobacco were hung, in order that, coming to reconnoiter, they would see that we were Spaniards and would come in search of us to get the tobacco. We traveled about six leagues this day.

On the 11th, before leaving the above-named place,[62] the governor sent two soldiers to see if the tobacco which we had left at the junction of the rivers was still there, and they said that the tracks left there indicated that the Indians had carried it off. We left the place and this day traveled about five leagues until midday, and found a crossing, although it was a difficult one. Two soldiers, having crossed in order to see if there was a good place to ford on the other side, came to another wide and deep creek which they could not ford.[63] That day we continued our journey upstream and arrived at a ravine which joins the river about ten leagues from where we left in the morning.[64] The way is very rough, owing to the hills, but in parts [it is] level. Many creeks are crossed, and ravines without water, most of them with rocky beds.

On the 12th, we left the above-named place in search of the said river [65] and traveled about twelve leagues.[66] The way is wooded and in places open. Every day we saw tracks and we always thought they were of bison, until this day, when about five in the afternoon, upon entering a thick wood, we saw a black Castilian bull. This made us think that all the tracks were made by the cattle which General Alonso de León left exhausted on the return from his first trip to Texas.[67]

On the 13th, after having left this place,[68] at about noon we reached the ford of the San Marcos river,[69] and until now we could not believe that it was the San Marcos, because everyone says that the San Marcos river enters the sea several leagues distant from the Guadalupe. The crossing is about eight to nine leagues from the above-named place.[70] The ford is wide and good, and at the entrance there is a thick wood of the same kind of trees that are downstream. This day we traveled in search of the Guadalupe river over the same road that leads to Texas and went about four leagues,[71] so that in all this day we covered thirteen. We stopped because a cloudburst caught us, which lasted unceasingly all night; and here as well as in San Antonio the thunderstorms are so frightful that all those who have experienced them in Spain, as well as in these parts, say that they have not seen any like them, for the shortest last six hours, with thunder pealing like harquebus-shots in battle.

On the 14th, we left this place and arrived about midday at the Guadalupe river. This day we traveled with great difficulty, since the road was very heavy owing to the heavy rain of the night preceding; the way is very level and with some ravines. We stopped at this river because we found it very swollen. A very extensive pasture

CHURCH OF SAN FRANCISCO DE LA ESPADA

is formed by these two rivers,[72] which is bordered by the hills that are about a half league from the road that leads to Texas.[73] Most of the land is overgrown with live oaks, poplars, elms, pecans, and oaks, and in all the land there are many grapes, larger than those of Castile, but, as I said, upon ripening they turn into wool. [There are also] many brambleberries. This day we traveled about four leagues.

On the 15th, we left the said place and traveled upstream with a desire to ford it or to reach its source. We traveled about three leagues[74] of very rugged land owing to the heavy woods and many rocks; and at the end of the three leagues two soldiers left for upstream to reconnoiter the land. They said that it could not be traveled because it is more wooded and contains more rocks, so that we returned to spend the night at the above-named crossing.[75] The woods consist of oaks and junipers, and the bank of the river is densely bordered by very tall savins. This day we traveled about six leagues.

On the 16th, we crossed the river with great difficulty; but first it is necessary for us to consider the things which occurred the day before. It so happened that after we had seen the swollen river and had investigated to see if it could be crossed or gone around, and had found no recourse whatsoever, the melancholy and sadness that fell upon the governor was so great that in his heart he felt no less than that the last days of his life had arrived; and thus, observing the obligations of a Catholic in such danger, he wanted to prepare himself, calling his secretary and dictating to him some things that had to be done if God should take him upon crossing this river. It so happened that, twenty-four buzzards having come to tarry close to where we were stopping, the governor asked the father chaplain, "Father, what are those birds looking for?" To which the father replied, "They may have come to make happy over the funeral rites of somebody present," at which the anguish was even greater, even before entering the water. He began, therefore, to cross with great difficulty, and the greatest fatality would have befallen us that can be imagined had not God and the most holy Virgin extended the arms of their omnipotence and mercy to protect and favor the governor against the extremely dangerous situation in which he found himself. He, having started to cross on the strongest horse that could be found, carried on the haunches the sergeant of the company. Upon arriving at the opposite bank, after having crossed most of the river, he reined the horse back, and, the current catching its haunches, it was swept downstream with both riders submerged and grasping the horse, for about half the distance of a musket-shot. At this place they came up still holding on to the horse, and, going down again, they lost their grasp on the horse, and the water carried them submerged for more than another half the distance of a musket-shot where they again arose. The anxiety they experienced may well be imagined, especially since the governor, who was dressed, did not know how to swim. And, although the said sergeant knew how to swim well, this would not have enabled him to rescue himself, because of the great force of the water, if here God had not performed a miracle through the intercession of His most pure Mother who provided them with two savin branches [76] to which they held on, and from there, because of the great depth, they were rescued by ropes. After this miraculous occurrence, I have asked the governor several times about the case, and he has always assured me that he does not know how he went [down the stream], whether under the water or over the water. The truth is that those who saw him say that he went downstream motionless, all of which proves that it was entirely a miracle, because the rescue could not have been attributed to natural causes, especially when the horse with the saddle nevermore turned up and the governor lost the buttons off his pants, thus forming a sort of ball and chain on his feet.[77] [For all of this] we thank unceasingly only God and His most holy Mother, and, moreover, we invoke their favor in the furtherance of this expedition and [place the] conquest under their charge. Furthermore, although [the governor] carried in his pocket a small silver box with the rosary and the prayer book in which the most holy Virgin is praised, they not only did not fall into the water when his pants came down, but the prayer book did not even get wet. This same day[78] we traveled about six leagues to a high hill where we stopped.

On the 17th, we arrived at the river of San Antonio, where the villa named Bexar stands, and found that nothing had occurred during our absence. From this day until the sixteenth of June, several scouting expeditions were made in which nothing in particular took place. During these days, also, things were begun to put the villa in shape. Maize was planted and lost, and the gardens were eaten by mice, which exist in great numbers. This day we traveled about nine leagues.

On the 16th of June, the governor sent three soldiers who understand farming to see if the water of the river could be drawn out, and they said they found it almost impossible, although they be paid their salaries in gold, owing to the many difficulties which the river and hills present.

On the 17th of June, the governor, finding himself unable to proceed with his trip, since he had not a single Indian, owing to the fact that the devil had them perverted and rebelling against God and against the King, left the villa of Bejar with several soldiers for the presidio of Rio Grande del Norte, in order to seek guides and to buy provisions so that he could reënter. We arrived at the said presidio of Rio Grande on the 21st day of the said month.

On the 27th of the said month, the reverend father president [79] of these missions of the Rio Grande del Norte left with nine soldiers and an *alférez* for the province of the Tejas, being sent by the governor in order to see if the cargoes which the father preacher Fray Miguel Núñez left near the Trinity river [80] were in the said place and to carry them to the missions of Tejas. In case the Indians might have stolen them, they took along new supplies which the governor donated from his private funds. The said governor also provided for the father president to regale and appease the Indians with tobacco, flannel, small blankets, and sackcloth. Before this, he had sent people out twice: once with four soldiers and the other time with thirteen and a lay-brother, to endeavor to get the said cargoes, and both times they returned because of not being able to cross the river which they call Colorado. [81]

On the 27th of August, [82] the father president of the Rio Grande [83] arrived at this villa of Bejar with the *alférez* and the nine soldiers, and with them the reverend father president of the missions of Texas [84] and Captain Domingo Ramón of that presidio of Texas. They brought the account that on the 21st of July the said father president of the Rio del Norte with the *alférez* and nine soldiers arrived at the lake which they call Santa Ana where the cargo had been left, and they found it in the same condition in which they [85] had left it on the 30th of March, and having fired the salvo with the joy of having found the cargo which they had judged lost, the said father president as well as the remaining soldiers affirm that they were answered with a salvo without

CHURCH OF SAN JUAN CAPISTRANO

knowing who did it, and this [occurred] with long inter-
missions. They searched but did not discover who could
have fired with great order the five shots, the number
they heard, and all wondered at the marvel. Four days
later the captain of Tejas and the reverend father president of the missions[86] arrived at this place on the lake.
They were coming in search of the same cargo since they
had finally received letters which the father preacher
Fray Miguel Núñez had left to be sent when he turned
back, and during the attempts which were made an Indian was drowned while crossing to give notice.[87] The day
on which all these people came here,[88] all the Indian
chiefs of the twenty-three nations which had been in revolt, arrived. They now came, enticed by the great
amount of clothing which the *alférez* had given them in
the name of the governor, in return for yielding to peace
and swearing obedience to his Majesty. The governor accepted their oath with much zeal, seeing them now sub-
dued, whereas a short while before they had been so
rebellious toward our holy mother Church and toward
the royal crown, because the devil had them so perverted
that this had obstructed the roads.

On the 3d of the month of September,[89] the governor,
proceeding with his good zeal, provided the reverend
father president of the missions of Texas with ten bales
of cloth, flour, horses, ten soldiers, sixty beeves, [all of]
which amounted to many pesos, to be distributed upon
the governor's arrival at the said province. Concerning
these gifts the said father has been very pleased as he
manifests by letter and certification to his Excellency [the
viceroy].

On the 5th of September, an Indian, named "El
Cuilón," whom all the nations recognize as a superior
and who was given the name Juan Rodríguez, was named
captain and governor of all the nations who are on the

road to the Tejas, and in witness of the fact that he was
given the requisite authority of lieutenant captain-general, the governor gave him his own baton of command.
Afterwards, the said governor and the reverend father
president of Texas left for the bay of Spiritu Santo,
with twenty-eight laden mules, sixteen laden with the
clothes and remaining needful things which the governor
gave to the reverend father president of Texas to carry
to the said province, and the other twelve with provisions
and dry goods which he takes along to distribute among
the Indians of the coast. Twenty-nine persons and the
father chaplain left with the governor at that time. With
the reverend father president [went] seventeen persons,
as well as another religious and three Texas Indians.
This day we left the said villa de Bejar, which remained
well supplied with needed things and defended by troops.
Both parties traveled together, with two hundred and
nineteen horses, and after having gone about a league,
we stopped at the spring of water where the river of
San Antonio rises.

On the 6th of the said month, the entire company left
the said place for the creek called Síbulo. The night before a conference was held of the governor, the three
religious, and the other principal officers, as to what was
to be done for the greater success of the expedition, and
all being together it was resolved that the entire company should go in search of the bay of Spiritu Santo, in
order that, the forces being joined, they might aid one another, and after having found the said bay, we might all
together take the road for Texas. This day we traveled
about six leagues.

On the 7th of the said month, we left the above-named
place and after having gone about three leagues, we left
the road we were following, which is the same which goes
to Tejas,[90] and heading straight to the east, we traveled

about five leagues, over some hills and all along the way through woods, in places thick with mesquites and some oaks. There are on the way some small hills and some short ravines, all of very loose soil. This day we came to a stop at a high hill which is on the bank of the Guadalupe river [91] in which the two branches now flow together.[92] There is here a waterfall which crosses the river from one side to the other. It is probably a little less than the distance of a musket-shot across. This day, at the order of the governor, Domingo Ramón went out with two soldiers to scout and reconnoiter the ground to be traveled the next day. Eight leagues were traveled.[93]

On the 8th of the said month, day of the nativity of the most holy Mary,[94] after the holy sacrifice of the mass had been celebrated, we left the said place in the direction of the east, downstream, through a wood so thick that it was necessary to go ahead with axes to open a path, and still it remained for us to open a way with our hands so that the laden mules might pass, which had to be led one by one by their halters. The wood is of mesquites, hackberries, much nopal,[95] and some mulberries and oaks. This day we traveled about five leagues and stopped on the bank of the same river.[96] The guide, who was a Moruame Indian,[97] fled today, and also another, a Payaya, and they carried off with them the horses on which they were riding.

On the 9th of the said month, before leaving the place, the governor sent two companions to examine the direction and way we were to take. Presently the governor mounted a horse to inspect a waterfall which is downstream [and] which crosses the entire river, and upon descending to the bank to examine it, the horse fell and left him on the ground. The camp left about eleven o'clock in the morning, heading east through woods, most of which were passable. We traveled close to the bank of the river, but it was necessary to leave it, because the woods were so thick that the father chaplain entangled himself in such a manner that he could not get out on any side. We went about four leagues, and a little while after we arrived at the place which was on the bank of the same river of Guadalupe,[98] the said companions returned, who said they had reconnoitered about three leagues ahead, and that upon exploring the river they had become stuck and one had been thrown, and that they had seen two Castilian bulls. There are also some turkeys in these woods.

On the 10th, we left the said place, the runners having first gone to reconnoiter, and we traveled downstream through woods and high rocky hills with oaks, live oaks, and pecans, always examining the river in order to find the falls and watering places. The river is densely overgrown with savins and pecans and is entirely navigable where it has been examined, for although two falls have been seen that cross it, they are low. This day on the road a Castilian bull was killed, and we stopped on the bank of the same river,[99] having traveled about six leagues.

On the 11th, we left the said spot and traveled east down the same river over hills and through woods very thick with oaks and live oaks. We crossed two dry creeks, and it was necessary in these as well as in the wood to open a road with axes in order to pass. This day we traveled about seven leagues and the junction of the three rivers was passed,[100] that is, of the Guadalupe,[101] the Alarcón,[102] and that which on the road that leads to Tejas is called the San Marcos.[103]

On the 12th, we left the above-named place and went east down the river, in which the three now run together, and at a matter of three leagues[104] we came out of the wood upon some very good and extensive plains, and a

little after having come upon the plains, we saw a small
hill where a cross with a pedestal of rock was placed.
This river is very deep and has a wide bed, so that water
cannot be drawn, and it is very delightful because it is
overgrown with savins, pecans, willows, and plum trees
which have plums already ripe and of a very good flavor.
This day about six leagues were traveled, and we stopped
on the bank of the same river.[105] This place was named
Real del Santísimo Nombre de María.

On the 13th, the river was crossed. The whole day was
spent doing this, because it was necessary to open ways
for a good distance on both sides of the river due to the
thick foliage of the trees. A raft of logs was made on
which the entire cargo was crossed, because the river was
swollen. On the opposite bank the camp was pitched,
after we had left a cross on a tree on either bank. It is
to be noted that at this point four rivers were crossed
which now run in one stream: the Guadalupe,[106] the one
called San Marcos on the road that leads to Tejas,[107] the
Alarcón, and the San Raphael.[108] The governor named
this place Real de la Exaltación de la Santísima Cruz.[109]

On the 14th, the camp went downstream through a
very thick wood of oaks and live oaks, and two creeks
that contain water, although not running, and that are
bordered by some willows. In places [we went through]
some small clearings. This day we traveled over some
hills in the direction of the northeast, and the expedition,
having traveled about five leagues this day, stopped at
some lakes of water that contain burdock and tule, with
a very tasty fruit.[110]

On the 15th, the camp left the above-named place, and
having gone a league we arrived at a miry creek where
it was necessary to repair the crossing. Beyond this there
is another large lake. About two leagues farther on we
came out of the wood upon open ground with low hills

and several clumps of live oaks. The camp stopped near a creek, after having gone about seven leagues.[111] Soon thereafter a squad of soldiers went out to scout and reconnoiter the ground.

On the 16th, we left the said place and headed in the direction of the northeast, quarter to the north and sometimes quarter to the east, over some very extensive, fertile, and delightful plains. We crossed this day on these plains three creeks of running water, and on one we stopped.[112] There are some clumps of live oaks. Eight leagues were covered, and as soon as the camp halted, four soldiers went out to reconnoiter and examine the ground.

On the 17th, day of the stigmata of my father Saint Francis,[113] the camp left this place while it was raining, and we traveled about three leagues over level and fertile ground, and two which in places were wooded although not thickly. [We passed] two running creeks and [came to] another on which the camp halted.[114] This creek had plenty of running water and was heavily wooded on both banks. This day five leagues were traveled.

On the 18th, the camp left the above-named creek, and after crossing it we entered a very thick wood. Afterward, we came out on a plain with some barren hills, and from there we entered another wood, much thicker, and upon leaving it, we came upon a marsh which is near the San Marcos river, which is that called the Colorado river on the road now used to go to Texas, but which is, in reality, the San Marcos.[115] All this day we traveled ten leagues toward the east-northeast.[116] Here the camp halted.

On the 19th, the camp having remained in the said place, the governor set out with seventeen men, the three religious, and an Indian, for the bay of Spiritu Santo, and at about a fourth of a league we entered a very de-

lightful valley which is bordered on the one side by the
San Marcos river [117] and on the other by a creek. It is
four leagues wide in its widest place, and in its narrow-
est two, and six leagues long. It was given the name of
El Valle de San Matheo. We arrived to rest at a small
wood which separates this valley from another which
follows, which has a length to a point which the river
forms of four leagues, and one cannot see to where the
plain reaches in breadth. It is all very fertile and un-
irrigated. The governor gave this second valley the name
of San Martín. This whole river is very beautiful and
bordered by poplars, plum trees, and other different trees.
This day we traveled about eleven leagues toward the
east-southeast.[118]

On the 20th, we left the said plain of San Martín and
entered another much more extensive, which, in what we
have traveled, is six leagues long, and, as far as the eye
can reach, is about twelve leagues in width. The governor
gave it the name of La Vega de San Isidro.[119] It is very
fertile, and very abundant in partridges. Today two
bison were killed, and in order that there might be time
to get the meat, we did not go forward and traveled only
six leagues toward the east-southeast. We halted on the
bank of the same river of San Marcos.[120]

On the 21st, after the holy sacrifice of the mass had
been celebrated, we continued our journey in the direction
of the east-southeast,[121] leaving the plain of San Isidro,
and in the same direction we entered another which was
given the name of San Joseph. It is seven leagues long
and ends in a creek from which another plain begins,
which was given the name of San Francisco, and soon
thereafter, in order to search for the river,[122] we changed
our direction, choosing east-northeast as far as a creek
with water on which we stopped, having traveled ten
leagues.[123]

On the 22d, we continued our journey in the direction of southeast, [124] and at about seven leagues we stopped to rest. Soon thereafter we proceeded in the same direction until we ran into a large inlet [125] which we were obliged to circle, because it was very wide and deep, and, it seems, navigable. We traveled four leagues to the south, the west, and in the direction of the north along a creek that contains some water, having gone this day twelve leagues. It happened that on this day, from noon until the evening prayers, the governor lay on a large snake at this place, without the reptile having moved, in spite of its known ferocity. This occurrence was taken to be almost a miracle.

On the 23d of the said month, we left the said creek, following the direction of the north in order to go around the head of the inlet. About half a league beyond we chose the direction of the south, and having gone five and a half leagues, we encountered another lake of salt water, [126] and having discovered that we had to return in order to go around it, we stopped to rest. After having gone around the head of it, we traveled about three leagues toward the southeast and came upon the bay of Spiritu Santo. [127] Having arrived on the beach, we went coasting along the entire shore of the sea to about two leagues to the southwest, [128] to an islet which may be about a fourth of a league long and a little more than the distance of a musket-shot across. This small island has some small nopal groves, some mesquites, and clumps of small oaks and chaparral. On the shore was a very thick beam, aground in the sand, and a short distance away in the water [there was] another, also aground. These [beams] are seen at low tide. Having arrived at the sea, we saw two Indians, and when we called them with signs, in order to talk to them about peace, they became afraid and threw themselves into the water and crossed the cove by swimming, which [cove] is a fourth of a league wide, more or less. We continued along the same shore on which, at about a league, we came unexpectedly upon a spring of fresh water which was very useful as we had no hope of finding any. There we halted. This spring of water rises in a clump of reeds near a small wood of mesquites, nopals, and some oaks and palms. The governor gave this spring of water the name of Santo Domingo. The position of the bay is from north to southwest, in the shape of a semicircle,[129] and [is] encompassed by an islet which seems to run from east to south for a distance of nearly three leagues, and from there the high seas begin.[130] Along the channel that runs north and northeast,[131] is seen a mouth through which the bays of Todos Santos and San Bernardo[132] join the sea. These bays are formed by the various inlets which we explored the preceding day. One can travel on them in canoes and reach fertile and very level lands. Judging by what was explored this time, the San Marcos,[133] in the examination of which we traveled almost to the sea, shows signs of entering the bay on the other side of the aforementioned islet, which forms an angle with the bay. In ascertaining these facts we traveled twelve leagues from the place where we stopped the day before.

On the 24th of the said month, before everything else, the holy sacrifice of the mass was celebrated by the father chaplain, Fray Francisco de Zelis, preacher and missionary of the mission of El Santissimo Nombre de Jesus del Peyote[134] of the province of Coahuila, and the said father is of the "Regular Observancia de Santiago de Jalisco del Orden Seraphico."[135] At this [mass] everybody was present. The muskets fired salvos while it was being celebrated, and mass being over voices were heard in the cove which faces east. The governor went with the Indian guide of the Asinay nation[136] who conducted us to the said bay, and also two soldiers, and upon nearing the said cove, they saw a canoe with several Indians paddling. Two remained on the shore. The Teja[137] Indian approached them cautiously, making signs of peace by which he detained them to speak to them. They made signs for us to leave. Nevertheless, they came closer and in a language somewhat familiar to them in which the Indian is proficient, he called to them and told them not to have any misgivings. They thus did as they were told, although very perturbed, and they embraced the governor. By this time the three religious and more soldiers had arrived, and going closer to the shore of the cove and alighting from our horses, we caressed them by embracing them and showed other customary signs of peace. Afterward, in the name of his Majesty, the said governor proceeded to distribute clothing and tobacco among the three who were present, and by means of the Indian guide who served as an interpreter, he told them to call the others who were in the canoe, who in all were four men, four women, and eight children, and to all of them he gave clothing and tobacco with which they were well pleased and showed their acknowledgment with a few dried fish which were all that they had with them at the time. They were given to understand that the intention of the Spaniards was to come and settle the said bay, and that they should give notice of the peace and friendship that were shown them to all those of their nation, which is called Caocose[138] and which is said to be very numerous and to inhabit the islets and shoals which surround the bay. They left very consoled and before going they told us of the place where Señor de la Sala with his Frenchmen had been, which is two leagues from the bay toward the west,[139] and we, having returned to the place, in the name of his Majesty, whom God keep, the said governor took lawful possession of all the bay, lakes, and neighboring lands in the manner required, and this act having been performed, we returned in the direction of the northeast by a straight route over level ground and we came to stop at a brook lined with poplars and willows and with pools of water, after having traveled ten leagues.

On Sunday, the 25th of the said month, after the holy sacrifice of the mass had been celebrated, we continued our journey in search of the camp, and we traveled until noon in the direction of the north to the bank of the river of San Marcos,[140] on which we halted after having gone sixteen leagues.

On the 26th, we continued a little in the direction of the north and the rest of the day toward the northwest, until we arrived at the place where the camp had remained, which, owing to the fact that the water had diminished, had moved another four leagues to the bank of the same river of San Marcos.[141] Because of this it was necessary for us to proceed this same day until we reached it. At the camp we found the entire nation of the Anames,[142] who had come in search of the governor to whom they gave [promises of] peace. From this a great deal was gained, because they are very proud Indians and because on other occasions they have been offered peace and have refused it, replying that they are as brave as the Spaniards. The whole crowd could not be counted because of its numbers. Here the governor, in the name of his Majesty, named as governor the oldest of them all. There was a storm here and a ray of lightning killed a very good horse of the father preacher Joseph Guerra, who is going as a missionary to Tejas. On the bank of this river there are also medlar[142a] trees like those of Spain. This day we traveled about eighteen leagues. They[143] are asking for a mission near the settlement of the French.

On the 27th, the camp was detained on this site, because the governor made a report to his Excellency giving him an account of all he has done to this day.[144]

On the 28th, after mid-day, the mail left for Mexico and the *alférez* of the company with eight soldiers [left] for the villa of Bejar in order to get provisions and other necessary things for the province of the Tejas. The governor set out with the camp for the said province. We crossed the river of San Marcos,[145] and for a distance of about two musket-shots it was necessary to make a way and to dismount. Soon thereafter we continued in the direction of the northeast through a very thick wood of oaks and over some hills, and the camp halted in a clearing near a running creek which was given the name of San Miguel,[146] because it was his eve and because the saint had been invoked to afford us water and a stopping place, since no one knew which way we were going. We went four leagues.

On the 29th, day of the glorious prince St. Michael, after the holy sacrifice of the mass had been celebrated, the camp left this site in the direction of the north through four leagues of oak forests,[147] and after having left the wood, we came upon the village of the Malleyes [148] so [suddenly] that the Indians were frightened, but after we called them with signs of peace, they stopped and presented us with medlars. After that we traveled four leagues over level hills, having gone altogether eight leagues this day.[149] This day a little before nightfall the sergeant of the company returned, who had gone with another soldier at the order of the governor to examine some smokes that had been seen. He brought six Indians of the Huyugan nation [150] with their chief, whom the governor received kindly and regaled with clothing and tobacco, and [the Indian chief] having slept there, very early in the morning the governor sent him to gather his people on the road.

RUINS OF PART OF THE BUILDINGS OF SAN JUAN CAPISTRANO

On the 30th of September, we left this creek, which was given the name of San Gerónimo,[151] and, while we were mounting the horses, many Indians of different nations arrived, who went forth with us, and at about three leagues it was necessary for us to stop owing to the multitude of Indians who had gathered. This was a day of much confusion, for as soon as we stopped, many more [Indians] arrived, and soon thereafter the governor ordered them to go for their women and children, and within three hours all of them had come together. After they had given promises of peace and obedience to his Majesty, the governor distributed clothing and tobacco to all, the men, women, and children being so many that they could not be counted. As we learned from the interpreter, six nations were united here with their chiefs, one [chief] of the Xanac nation,[152] another of the Emet nation,[153] another of the Too nation,[154] another of the Malleyes nation, another of the Huyugan nation, [and] another of the Curmicai nation,[155] and all together asked for a mission and indicated a site which was near the river of Guadalupe on a small hill where we put a cross when we passed there on the 12th of this month, because they say a good spring of water is there. They now live in some very pleasant glens with many trees, mostly live oaks, oaks, and pecans, and very abundant medlar trees. We traveled only three leagues.[156]

On the first day of October, we left this place in the direction of the north in order to go around some extensive forests which were there. Soon thereafter we took the direction of the northeast through some very pretty ravines and level ground. This day three bison were killed and ten leagues were traveled, and the camp halted on a creek with pools of water.[157]

On the 2d of October, we left this spot through a very thick wood, so that it was necessary to clear a path in order to pass, and [we encountered] many creeks which cost us sufficient trouble to cross. This wood is composed of oaks, live oaks, *tejocotes*,[158] and many medlar and plum trees. This day we traveled eight leagues in the direction of the north.[159]

On the 3d of the said month, we left this place, which consists of some pools, and traveled about a league through a wood of plum trees of different colors and medlar trees. Soon thereafter we came into the open, and in places [there were] some small woods. We traveled always in the direction of the north, until arriving at the ordinary road which is used today for Tejas, half a league before reaching the river[160] which joins the Colorado,[161] having first passed through some large and small Indian villages where there was a cross. This day very many bison were seen and five were killed. The governor gave this place the name of the Camp of San Francisco, and we traveled eight leagues.

On the 4th of October, the day of my seraphic father and patriarch, St. Francis,[162] the camp did not leave this place where three masses were said, and afterwards the men went to clear the road in order that the laden mules could pass. This day six bison were killed.

On the 5th, we left this camp in the direction of the east-northeast, and half a league from the place we arrived at the first branch[163] of the real Colorado river,[164] which is this one and which runs in two branches, and from one branch to the other there is a league and a half of very thick woods of mulberries, pecans, black poplars, wild grapes, and Castilian poplars, very high and very thick. We then crossed the other branch of the said Colorado[165] and after that we traveled in the same direction through some clearings and small woods. The camp halted at a creek which contains water in pools. This [place] was given the name of Camp of Los Angeles.[166] We traveled seven leagues.

On the 6th of the said month, we left this place and a short while after having begun traveling, we had a storm with much thunder and rain, which obliged us to stop after having gone a league, and we remained all day on the bank of a creek near a wood, which contained rainwater. This day five bison were killed.

On the 7th, we left this creek in the direction of the east-northeast, and at four leagues we arrived at a stream which is called Corpus Christi,[167] having first crossed many creeks with rainwater, and afterwards in the same direction we traveled another five leagues. We crossed the creek of San Buenaventura,[168] and arrived to stop near the bank of the lake of Santa Ana.[169]

On the 8th of the said month, we left this lake in the direction of the east-northeast, over level ground with little wood and some clearings and creeks, and we came to halt near a spring of water which is called Santa Clara.[170] We stopped in a small wood of live oaks, which was given the name of the Camp of the Crosses, because of our having placed many on the said oaks. We traveled ten leagues.

On the 9th of the said month, we left the Camp of the Crosses in the direction of the east-northeast, and at about three leagues we arrived at the lake of San Christoval and immediately thereafter we crossed a creek of running water. At [a distance of] another league is the lake of San Luis Obispo[171] and the creek of Santa Rosa. This day we went seven leagues, through woods [and over] hills covered with pecan trees, and stopped on a small hill. This day the ground was very heavy, because it had rained.

On the 10th, we left the above-named place in the direction of the east-northeast, [traveling] through clear woods and always through water, since there was a continuous lake owing to the great deal it had rained. We passed through this lake for the five leagues we traveled until we arrived at the river of the most holy Trinity,[172] which we found very swollen, and we halted on its bank. This afternoon, in order to make a canoe, a log was cut down which had a circumference of three *brazas*.[173]

On the 11th, work on the canoe was continued, but seeing the great delay, because of the tools being bad, the governor decided that a raft of logs should be made. This was done, and today the governor, the three religious, and half of the cargo were crossed. While crossing, the father chaplain and another religious were in great danger, when the raft almost sank. Most of the cargo, half of the people, and all the horses remained on the other bank.

On the 12th, the cargo continued to be crossed, and as soon as it was finished, the horses were driven into the water. Since the river was very swollen, nine horses were drowned, and we were thankful to God that not all of them were. This day the father president of Tejas went on ahead, and the camp remained on the bank of the river.

On the 13th, we left the said river in the direction of the east-northeast, over a very hilly land with a great deal of forest of pecans, pines, [and] chestnuts with very delicious, although small, nuts. The pecans were so plentiful that they covered the ground. We arrived at a creek which was given the name of Santa Coleta. We stopped after having gone twelve leagues.[174]

On the 14th, Friday, the governor left the camp of Santa Coleta in the direction of the northeast. The way consists of valleys, ravines, and clearings with open woods of oaks and many pecans, and at a distance of four leagues a very extensive clearing was reached along whose border from west to east flows a permanent creek. In the northern part of the said clearing there are two lakes, and it is the place where the settlement of the year ninety was located.[175] From here [we continued] in the same direction of the northeast, through woods somewhat clear and over some hills and ravines. We inspected the spot where, in the expedition of the year '16, the presidio stood for the first time.[176] After crossing a somewhat swollen creek which is permanent,[177] and traveling through clearings and much reed-grass and open woods, we came upon the mission of Our Father San Francisco,[178] where the governor was received with great joy and ringing of bells by the father missionaries and by the Indians of that tribe with gifts of their usual food. The said governor regaled the Indians and explained to them the purpose of his coming and the desire of our Catholic king and lord for the conversion of their souls. [He told them] that he wanted them all to congregate in order that they might live in a civil community. This they promised to do but [the plan] could not be executed, because the Indians were about to go in search of bison meat, the crop having been short this year. The governor gave this mission the name of Pueblo de San Francisco de Balero. It now remains with two religious of the college of Santa Cruz.[179] The Christians who have been baptized in danger of death are twenty. Here Friday was spent after we had traveled twelve leagues.[180]

On the 15th, in the direction of between northeast and east-northeast, having passed a creek of water which is followed by plains for more than two leagues and at intervals by open woods of pecans and oaks, we encountered other larger plains, until through open woods and a great deal of reed-grass, the creek[181] near the mission of La Purísima Concepción[182] was reached. Here a great number of Indians, very joyful, came forth to meet the said

governor, and on the banks was Captain Domingo
Ramón[183] with some soldiers, and all [having come] together, they fired a salvo and walked to the mission,[184]
where the father president of La Santa Cruz (who had
gone on ahead four days before) was waiting, and with
two other religious they received the said governor in
the best manner that the country permits, the bells and
musket-shots making the reception more joyful. Later the
reception of the said governor was continued on the part
of the Indians according to their custom, and it was in
this manner: the straw house having been made ready
where he was to lodge, they took him from his horse,
and having placed him on his feet, an Indian chief took
his sword and pistols, and another took him by the
shoulders and another by the feet, and in this manner
they arrived at the said door of the house, where, while
he was standing, they washed his face and hands gently
and dried them with a cloth which they had requested
for that purpose. They carried him in, two Indian chiefs
holding him by the shoulders, and after they had
seated the governor on a small bench, they gave him
the pipe of peace, and after having reciprocally performed this ceremony, they gave him to understand how
greatly they enjoyed his coming, for which they had
wished for a long time because of the news that the father
missionaries had given them. The said governor pointed
out to them the intention of his Majesty, and he came at
his command in order to confirm them in their good peace
and friendship with all the Spaniards. He ordered them
to make a house in which he could live during the time
that he might remain in this province, and they promised
to do it with all promptness. This day eight leagues were
traveled from the pueblo de San Francisco Balero.[185]

The Indians of the tribes which had assembled spent
the 16th and 17th in building the house, which they did

in accordance with their custom, of timber, in a pyramidal form, covered with grass, and this day, in the afternoon, they called together all the chiefs in order to make his reception more solemn. They celebrated it that night in the following order: the Indians having dressed in gala form with their hides, and all the people—men, women, and children—having assembled, a great bonfire was [kindled] in the patio of the house, in front of which they put a small wooden bench and skins of bison for carpets. After the principal Indians and chiefs had entered the house, they took the governor by his arms and with great care placed on his head some feathers from the breasts of white ducks and on his forehead a strip of black cloth which fell to his cheeks. Then they placed him on the skins, a leading Indian who was seated on the small bench and who was holding him by the shoulders, serving him as a thing to lean on. At this time the drum or kettledrum (which they make of a large water-jug, covered with a stretched and dampened skin) commenced to resound, accompanied by the timbrels and singing of the whole multitude. The people, arranged in order, sang while being seated in their manner, the men being uniformly separated from the women and children, who, without disagreeing one point in their voices, made a gentle, although coarse harmony. Four bonfires were made by the Indians, which make a remarkable light, and the Indian superintendents carried in their hands torches of burning reeds and walked about very carefully in order to keep all the Indians in order. From time to time a leading Indian of the proctors who are in the settlement interrupted the singing, and standing before the governor, he began his discourse, telling [him] of the great pleasure with which they received him into their lands and all the Spaniards and fathers whom they already had, and that thenceforward their friendship

and relations would be closer, and that since he[186] had
permitted to let himself be received according to their
custom, they no longer looked upon him as a stranger
but as if born among them. [They said that] they received him as their chief, and in consequence of this they
would help him and his people in anything that might
present itself, and that they were asking him to do the
same, defending them with the Spaniards against the
enemies who were harassing them. [In answer] to this,
his Lordship, by means of an interpreter, promised to
perform for them all the good services that he could, and
that this courtesy was showing it and had shown it in
the name and person of his king and lord, to whom, he
declared, they should be always grateful and submissive
because of the great deal that he had spent and was
spending in loving them. The discourses having ended,
the singing and shouting continued very gaily and joy-
fully, all the Indians saying in their language that they
would do as they were told and took it as very good and
acceptable. The other proctors were doing the same
thing in the name of all the nations, those whom each
nation had in the presence of the governor exchanging
places so that all would have a part in the ceremony.
This function lasted until three in the morning, thus giving all those at the assembly an opportunity to catch a
little rest.

Tuesday, the 18th, all the chiefs of the settlements of
La Concepción de Agreda[187] and San Joseph de Ayamonte[188] assembled, and by means of their spokesman,
renewed the agreements of their recognition with the
governor, who repeated his mission in the name of his
Majesty; and after they had spent a long time with their
discourses, alternating their pipe of peace with the con-
versation, the governor gave them tobacco and a goodly
portion of clothing of all colors, which they were to dis-

tribute among themselves. This the spokesmen adjusted with due promptness, leaving the chiefs of both nations and other chiefs who happened to be present from the tribe of the Caudachos [189] very contented. The latter pointed out that they desired to receive the Spaniards in their villages.[190] This day all the Indians came in marching order, firing their muskets with such precision that it seemed that they had been well disciplined in the militia; and as was noticed by all, the governor was received with shots from more muskets than the said governor had on his side,[191] because a great number of them had been introduced among the Indians in the neighborhood of the French, who gave them to the Indians in exchange for horses and skins.

On Wednesday, the 19th, in order to increase the new Christianity of this province, the governor acted as godfather to three creatures, whom the father voluntarily offered for holy baptism, which was performed with the greatest solemnity possible, many Indians attending the function. To this was added the ringing of bells and firing of muskets, making the concourse more joyful. With these the baptized in the village of La Concepción de Agreda amount to sixty-two. Later the governor proceeded to distribute clothing to all of the family of those baptized, among whom is found the sagacious Indian woman interpreter [192] who at the persuasion of the said governor came to live with her entire family near the village. The village has another five houses near by and will serve as a nucleus for remaining ones to come, which the governor does not doubt he will bring about, provided a new force of Spaniards comes in.

On the 20th, 21st and 22d, Indians did not cease assembling from all the settlements. They came and went in order to see the said governor, some bringing gifts of things that they use in their meals, because of which they left again contented and remunerated.

On the 23d, all the chiefs of the settlement of Agreda assembled, saying that only those of the said settlement wished to give him a feast in the same manner as in the first reception. They came from all the houses, offering their baskets of meal and other edible things and some tanned deer-skins, which was all that they had at that time; and this day with new demonstrations they explained clearly that they had now received the said governor as *Cadi A Ymat*,[193] that this term means Great Captain, and that they looked upon him as if they had created him. The function lasted until nearly daybreak, so that there was only a short time for rest.

On the 24th, 25th and 26th, the time was spent in distributing clothing and the other things that had been brought for all the settlements, and at the same time the supplies [were distributed] that had been brought especially for the soldiers who are in this province. During all these days and the preceding ones the governor made a special effort to see if there was any clothing of that which the French had introduced in the past year, and he found that a long time before his arrival the same Frenchmen had taken it back to their settlement of Los Nachitochos [sic], and thus he did not have to do anything in regard to this matter.

On the 27th, 28th and 29th, the only memorable thing was that some Indians of the Biday nation[194] assembled with their chief and some women and children, all of whom the said governor ordered regaled, and the said chief, in the name of those of his nation, said that they would assemble in the settlement which might be assigned to them and at the time that might be wished. The said nation is extremely numerous and extends for [a distance of] three days on the road from this pueblo of La Concepción de Agreda to the coast where other nations are [living] who are friends of the Tejas. The chief of the Bidais was determined to go to Mexico, because the governor had told him to, but he is not going because he is ill.

On the 31st, the governor acted as godfather to a creature who was solemnly baptized, and he gave it things with which to dress. Later his Lordship went to visit the mission of San Joseph de los Nasones,[195] which lies to the north and northeast. He was received by the religious with great joy and ringing of bells, and the Indians on their part joined in the celebration, and there the remainder of the day was spent inspecting what there was near the mission, which has the name of pueblo of San Joseph de Ayamonte. Thirty-one persons have been baptized in this mission. Two religious of the college of Santa Cruz de Querétaro remain in it.

On the 1st of November, even in spite of the great cold and the norther that was blowing, the said governor went to investigate the ridge of mountains which can be seen from the mission at a distance of a league, and having walked over all of it in order to see if he might find some veins of metal, he found only a great deal of rock which they call *quemazón,*[196] and this procedure [having been] completed, he returned to the pueblo where he spent that night.

On Wednesday, the 2d, he made his return trip to the pueblo of La Concepción de Agreda. Nothing unusual happened this day.

On the 3d, preparations were made to go and visit the missions that remained, and this day [the governor] received letters from the French who are in Nachitochos, [in answer to] those which the governor had courteously sent them, and they showed in the said letters that in everything that was presenting itself, the two crowns were acting with entire urbanity and friendly relations and in harmony.[197]

On the 4th, the governor departed and with him the reverend father president of the missions of Santa Cruz and eight soldiers. [Traveling] in the direction of the northeast,[198] passing several villages of Asinais Indians that are intermediate, and [going through] country [that consists] of open woods of pecans, some pines and oaks, and in places through clearings and ravines, they arrived at the mission of Nuestra Señora de Guadalupe[199] where the principal minister was very near the last days of his life. They were well received by his companion, with ringing of bells and firing of muskets, and having spent the rest of the day inspecting the neighborhood of that place, the governor named it pueblo of Nuestra Señora de Guadalupe de Alburquerque.[200] Those who have been baptized are twenty-seven. This day about ten leagues were traveled.[201]

On the 5th, traveling in the same direction,[202] although making detours in all directions owing to the winding of the roads, and passing through ravines and open woods of pecans, oaks, pines, and some small creeks and clearings, they arrived at a river which the said governor named Todos Santos.[203] It carried quite a bit of water, and on the other side camp was made that night. This day we traveled about fifteen leagues.[204]

On Sunday, the 6th of the present month, they left the said river, and the father president went to say mass at the mission of Dolores[205] which is more than six leagues distant.[206] There, the said father president having arrived beforehand, he and the most reverend father Fray Antonio Margil[207] received the said governor by singing the Te Deum Laudamus and by having prayers in the church. And mass having been said, they spent that day in discussing what was necessary for the welfare of the province. It would be necessary to reconstruct this mission of the tribe of the Ays.[208] The governor named it pueblo of Nuestra Señora de los Dolores de Benavente. This nation is numerous and twenty persons have been baptized.[209] And this day about six leagues were traveled.[210]

The 7th was also spent in conferring on this same subject.[211]

On the 8th, the governor left for the other mission, and [traveling] in the direction of the east and northeast, [passing through] ravines and clearings and many [groves of] pecans and in some places pines and [through] some permanent creeks, they arrived at a very spacious clearing. On its borders [flowed] a creek with good water, where they made camp, after having traveled fourteen leagues.

On the 9th, [going] almost in the same direction, and through woods which for the greater part were of pine groves and oaks, they arrived at a river with many savins, which the governor gave the name of river of San Francisco de Sabinas,[212] and although it carried quite a bit of water, it offered a place to ford, and having passed many tributaries on both banks, which in the winter, upon leaving the said river, are very difficult to pass, we went on about seven leagues farther, having traveled this day about thirteen leagues.

On the 10th, [traveling] in about the same direction, in places [through] pine groves [and through] many clearings, creeks, [and groves of] pecans, we reached the mission of San Miguel de los Adaes [213] at about three o'clock in the afternoon. The father president accompanied the missionary religious in singing the Te Deum Laudamus, and the governor was received with great joy. This mission was named pueblo of San Miguel de Cuellar [214] by the governor. Here seventeen persons have been baptized. We traveled fifteen leagues this day.[215]

On the 11th, the governor dispatched his sergeant and another soldier to the settlement of the French [216] so that they might observe cautiously all that might be there, and in the meantime his Lordship went to examine a lake [217] which is about two leagues from the said pueblo and comes from the river of San Andres de los Cabdachos.[218] This river has a very large waterfall, and, according to a report which the Indians made there, [the lake has] a circumference of more than fifty leagues, is of fresh water, and on its banks [are] a great many medlar trees. The Indians travel on it in their canoes because it is entirely navigable and because one can go by it to Cabdachos,[219] and by way of the part where it returns to join the said river, one can navigate to Los Nachitochos and Mobile, because the said river, which the French call La Rivera or Red River, at eighty leagues enters the river of La Palizada which the French call Mississippi. This lake, with the rest of the adjacent land having been examined, the governor went to regale the chiefs of those tribes with clothing, and this day all that there was in that country and territory was reported.

On the 12th, the sergeant and the other soldier returned from Nachitochos and reported that the French had a simple stockade and [that] their houses [were] of wood and the roofs of the bark of trees, and that the number of French people did not reach twenty persons. Because of this, the governor, heeding the fact that all of these lands are the patrimony of his king and lord, had the desire to tell the said Frenchmen to abandon the place, or in some other way to make them abandon it, provided the orders of the most excellent viceroy would not serve as an obstacle. To this all the religious remonstrated several times, and in accordance with the order [to the governor from the viceroy], it was resolved to leave until further notice from his Excellency what they might henceforth decide [to be] best and most advantageous for the peace of the crowns and the welfare of this entire province.[220] At the same time he took particular notice of two Frenchmen present among the Cabdachos, who are the ones through whose hands the French acquire slaves and other things of that land from the Indians. Since the Indians are so interested in muskets, powder, bullets, and clothing, which they exchange for young slaves, wars are maintained and even brought about among the Indians themselves, causing many tribes to be destroyed who would otherwise be converted to Christianity. There is sufficient proof of this.

At the same time, the governor had private information that on the Missouri river, which according to reports is about two hundred leagues from the said river of Cabdachos, near [a place] where this Missouri river enters the Palizada, there is a rich mine. That the metal is rich is known by the fact that they cannot found the metal for bullets, and the said governor has a person who will take him to the said mine. In these regions of the Tejas no vein or land has been discovered that might appear to be mineralized.

During this [journey] the governor tried to discharge the commission which was committed to him, and all that is executed in this diary recognizes that it has been the powerful hand of God through the intercession of His most pure Mother, that has lent him life, rescuing him from a known shipwreck, giving into his hands the many nations that remain pacified, making the weather serene, which never has been known [to be] so favorable, and, with such a small number of soldiers, allowing him to travel through such different lands without great injury. For this he wishes that all give the honor and glory to

such a Sovereign Queen [as she] who has been guide in
his wanderings, ship in his shipwrecks, consolation in the
forced hardships of such a long road, and a mediator
who has removed all difficulties. Because of this, the said
governor was motivated to acknowledge the recognition
by celebrating with a sung mass and sermon [and] with
the attendance of numerous clergymen, a solemn feast to
Our Queen and Lady, most holy Mary, through whose
prayers this province hopes for its greatest growth.
Amen.

The governor, having brought this undertaking to a
close, and having dispatched mail to his Excellency giving
him an account of all that had been executed, and it being
necessary for him to return to the new villa of Bejar in
order to take charge of its development, left the said
province on the twenty-eighth of November for the referred to villa of Bejar, having first named a lieutenant
in the province of the Tejas and having completed the
company of twenty-five men with men whom he had
brought, leaving seven[221] with all [their] arms and
horses, together with thirty more horses of those which
the said governor [had] received to the account of his
Majesty, for the remaining soldiers, and a stock of
clothing for the said company at the prices of the province of Coahuila. And having arrived on the twenty-ninth
of the said [month] at the place called San Pedro de los
Navidachos,[222] which is the place where the Spaniards
settled in the year '90, and the said governor having
[had] information of a bell which had been hidden when
the Spaniards left, he ordered the camp to go on and for
the soldiers to search for the said bell, promising a prize
to the one who should find it, and it having been found,
his Lorship designated it for the said villa of Bejar. It
weighs six *arrobas*.[223]

And having arrived on the following day at a creek

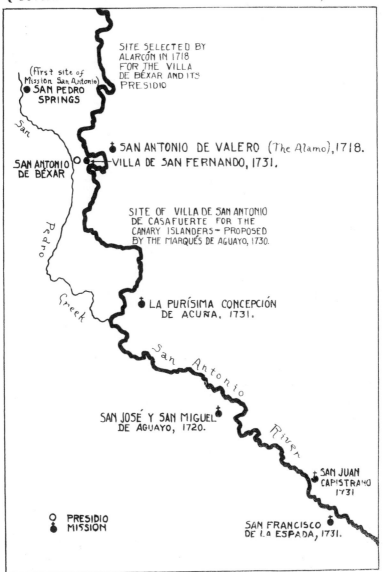

(First site of
Mission San Antonio)
● SAN PEDRO
  SPRINGS

SITE SELECTED BY
ALARCÓN IN 1718
FOR THE VILLA
DE BÉXAR AND ITS
PRESIDIO

San

● SAN ANTONIO DE VALERO (The Alamo), 1718.
SAN ANTONIO ○ VILLA DE SAN FERNANDO, 1731.
DE BÉXAR

Pedro

SITE OF VILLA DE SAN ANTONIO
DE CASAFUERTE FOR THE
CANARY ISLANDERS — PROPOSED
BY THE MARQUÉS DE AGUAYO, 1730.

Creek

● LA PURÍSIMA CONCEPCIÓN
    DE ACUÑA, 1731.

San Antonio

SAN JOSÉ Y SAN MIGUEL ●
    DE AGUAYO, 1720.

River

● SAN JUAN
  CAPISTRANO
    1731

○ PRESIDIO
● MISSION

SAN FRANCISCO ●
DE LA ESPADA, 1731.

SAN ANTONIO, 1718-1731

near the river of the most holy Trinity, we found it so swollen that it was necessary to cross it on rafts, because it was so wide that it measured more than the distance of a musket-shot across. Having crossed the creek, we found ourselves stranded, because the said river was flooded beyond measure. In this place many hardships were suffered during the delay of twenty-two days with rain on most of these, and after we had decided to cross by means of rafts, when [we launched] the first one, on which went the silver service of the governor, the kitchen, the clothing, and the cook, the whole thing was sunk, nothing having been saved except the negro cook.[224] The crossing of the river was later made by raft, although the salvaging of the silver could not be effected. We continued our journey always in the direction of the west, and we crossed the river Colorado,[225] which contained quite a bit of water, and that which they call Puerco, with much more [water], and many other creeks. Later we crossed the *monte grande*.[226] The name fits it, since it is necessary to bring a guide in order to go through it, because it is so wooded and entangled with *cocolmecates*. After this many creeks are encountered, and the largest of them is that of Las Animas,[227] that is, to the river of San Marcos.[228] Soon thereafter we passed this river in three branches.[229] After this the Garrapatas River [230] is encountered, and soon thereafter that of San Raphael [231] which is followed by that which they used to call San Marcos.[232] The governor gave it the name of Los Inocentes,[233] and it has its source three-fourths of a league from the ford, toward the north.[234] Later the river of Alarcón [235] was passed, which carried more water than usual, and it was noticed that the bough of the savin which the governor seized when he found himself in the said river in danger of drowning,[236] was dry, the whole tree being green. After that the river of Guadalupe [237] was crossed, which has its origin a fourth of a league from the ford, in the direction of the north.[238] Soon thereafter [we reached] the river of San Antonio, near this villa of Bejar in which nothing unforeseen whatsoever had happened during the time that the governor was absent. There were many Indians of the three following tribes in the mission of San Antonio de Balero, to wit: Xarames,[239] Payayas, and Pamayas.[240] They had been brought to the said mission by the lieutenant whom the said governor had left with orders that thus it should be done. On the day following his arrival, the governor distributed among these nations a great deal of baize cloth, sackcloth, little blankets and tobacco, and soon thereafter the governor went to name one of the highest chiefs of these three nations as governor of all of them, and at the same time, choosing men from the highest chiefs, he appointed the *alcaldes, justicia* and *regimiento,* so that thus they might enter better into the art of government, the said mission having been put into complete condition. These heathen show signs of having been taught, for at the sound of the bell they assemble for prayer with great haste and energy, for which thanks must be given to God.

On the 12th of the said month of January, although the weather was very severe and unusual, the governor gave orders to begin with all assiduity the construction of the canals for both the villa and the said mission of San Antonio de Balero. This work was continued the remainder of the said month, in which time they were built in good state and shape, so that this year a fine crop of corn, beans, and other grains which the governor ordered brought in from the outside is expected. At the same time, he had grapevines and fig trees and various seeds of fruits brought in, [seeds] of cantaloupe and watermelon, as well as of pumpkin, chile, and all the remaining necessary things. At the same time he ordered hogs brought in for breeding, and much cattle and small livestock, goats as well as sheep, so that the said villa finds itself supplied with all the necessary implements, livestock, and munitions, without lacking anything whatsoever.

On the 29th of this month of January, the governor received notice that the French captain Leonís,[241] who was in prison in the City of Mexico, had escaped from the said court and directed his way toward the province of the Tejas. In accordance with this notice and in order to avoid the harm that might result from this, the governor dispatched a person of his confidence to give him an account of the condition of the twenty-three nations of the Ranchería Grande [242] or [to see] if perhaps the said French captain had disturbed them, and [his man] having made this investigation, the governor found that all the nations were quiet, peaceful, and calm, without the least change, since they had not taken notice of the said Frenchman because they had seen him in a poor condition, and they were interested in making a profit.

This same day, an Indian of the nation of the Pamayas arrived to speak with the governor and to bring him some red vermilion or red ochre from a mine that he said he knew of and which was in the direction of the north. In this mine, he asserted, according to his mode of explaining himself by signs and by talking, there were rocks of different types of metals. In accordance with this, the governor, having given the most excellent Marqués de Balero, viceroy of this New Spain, information of all that had happened since the 24th of December of the past year, informed him also of the intention that he had of ordering this mine to be examined, and with the mail that he dispatched on the 4th of February he remitted to his Excellency a sample of the referred to vermilion.

During this interval the reverend father Antonio de San Buenaventura y Olivares [243] also arrived at his mission of San Antonio de Balero, and he brought with him two Frenchmen to work in the said mission, and the governor, recognizing that from this [procedure] grave injuries might result and that it was plainly against the orders of the said most excellent lord, ordered them arrested, and thus they remained until the said reverend father bound himself in writing to restore them to the spot whence he had brought them. And his Excellency was informed [of this].

On the 6th of February, the governor ordered that the referred to mine of vermilion be examined, for which purpose he dispatched a squad of soldiers in charge of the sergeant and they left in search of the said mine. They reached it after having traveled about eighty leagues, a little more or less, and it was recognized to be the range of mountains that they call La Plata, which, according to what they say, is about three and a half days from the villa of Santa Fee [sic] of New Mexico. And having inspected the part from which the Indians take vermilion and other colors for painting themselves, they found rocks that seem to be metal. For this reason the governor remitted a portion to his Excellency in order to know if it has any quality, although the said rocks are from the surface of the ground. Not very far distant, in the extent of the said range, others of lesser quantity glisten in the sun, owing to the great amount of white gravel that is among them, and with the reflection of the rays of the sun it looks like silver. A great number of Indians went with the said squad whom the governor sent in order that they might take cognizance of everything, and with this is ended this diary. All is given for the greater honor and glory of God and of his most holy Mother. Amen. Jesus, Mary, and Joseph.

All that is contained in this diary I certify to be according to and as is contained therein. As an eye-witness [and] because of having been chaplain of this entire undertaking, and because therefore it is the truth, I signed it at this said villa of Bejar on the tenth of February of the year one thousand, seven hundred, and nineteen.

FRAY FRANCISCO DE CÉLIZ
(*Rubric*)

NOTES TO THE DIARY

1. The names New Philippines and Province of Texas were interchangeable. "The original Texas was the territory of the Hasinai (Texas) Indians, between the Trinity and the Red rivers, and included much of what is now Louisiana. Early in the eighteenth century the boundaries were extended westward to include the settlements on the San Antonio River and Matagorda Bay. With the founding of the province of Nuevo Santander, in 1746, the western boundary of Texas was officially fixed at the lower Medina River. . . ." Bolton, *Texas in the Middle Eighteenth Century,* p. 1; see also Introduction, note 5, and Hackett, *Pichardo's Treatise,* I, 402.

2. Probably by means of the ford called "Paso de Francia," situated about five miles from the mission of San Juan Bautista del Rio Grande and about thirty miles downstream from modern Eagle Pass. Today it bears the name of Guerrero, Coahuila. The ford, described by Father Morfi in his *Viage de Indios,* for more than two centuries remained the preferred ford of the expeditions that entered Texas from Coahuila. *Documentos para la Historia de Mexico,* Tercera Serie, Tomo Primero, pp. 446–447; see also Introduction, note 3. Santa Anna used the ford in 1836 when he entered Texas to quell the revolution. Where it received its name is a mystery, but it may have been given that name because it was used by the expedition which in 1689 went in search of La Salle's colony or because the Frenchman St. Denis arrived there from Louisiana in 1714.

3. The Spanish word is *real*—a site on which stands the tent of the king or of the general of a king, and also a site on which an army is encamped. In New Spain the word was applied mainly to mining camps, as, for example, the famous Real del Monte in Pachuca, which name persists today; but it was also used in regard to points occupied by soldiers in regions inhabited by nomadic Indians. In the text the word *real* is translated as camp or expedition.

4. The meaning here may be that the governor was on the south bank of the Rio Grande, whereas the camp had crossed the river. Since no directions are given until the entry for May 8th, we are at a loss to know exactly which route the expedition took. Our estimates will be mere conjectures. Even with the directions and leagues later given, our estimates can be only approximate, since the names of the streams, lakes, and other landmarks are very confusing, and the number of leagues stated cannot always be depended on, for the expedition often became lost. The direction at this time was probably northeast, and Las Rosas de San Juan must have been a place seven leagues northeast of the mission of San Juan Bautista. The name of Las Rosas de San Juan is derived from a very common, small white wild-flower, which grows in most of Mexico and a large part of the southwestern United States. It's botanical name is *Houstonia longiflora,* and it is also known as Flor de San Juan. Large

bunches of this flower may be had at a very cheap price in the markets of Mexico City. See Irene Elena Motts, *Nociones de Botánica,* pp. 242–244, Tlalpan-Mexico, 1931.

5. Literally: Camp of the Crow. De León's diary, entry for Saturday, April 1, 1689, says: "We crossed the river [the Rio Grande] and went about one league north, to avoid some ravines and low hills. Afterward we went mostly northeast, until we reached some pools, five leagues away. We named these *El paraje de los Cuervos,* because more than three thousand crows appeared at nightfall." West, "De León's Expedition," p. 203.

6. A league is 4.190 meters or 2.60199 miles. There are several leagues, but in Spanish America the judicial league is almost always meant.

7. Las Rosas de San Juan.

8. *Carrizo* is a reed found in and around water holes. If the direction here was northeast, this place may have been near present Byrds, Texas. If the direction was more east-northeast, it may have been near modern Carrizo Springs, Texas.

9. It is interesting to note the interest of the Spaniards in streams and water-holes that might be used for irrigation. Similar comments are made at almost every stream.

10. El Carrizo.

11. This is evidently meant for Carabanchel and the stream received its name from a municipality four kilometers from Madrid, Spain. See *Enciclopedia Universal Ilustrada Europeo-Americana,* XI, 624. No directions are given, but the creek may have been one of the small streams near present Byrds. If this be the case and Carrizo Springs (Texas) was his previous stop, Alarcón must have changed his course to the northwest.

12. Probably the same tribe as that known also as Pacuache, Pakawa, and Pacao. This tribe was living near the San Antonio river when the missions were moved there from East Texas in 1730–1731. According to Fray Espinosa they were a very docile tribe. Hodge, *Handbook,* II, 191–192.

13. The creek called Caramanchel.

14. Literally: The Pools of the Live-oaks. No directions are given, but this may have been one of the small lakes near present Crystal City and Byrds. An *encino* or *encina* is an evergreen or live oak, to distinguish it from the roble, or the oak that sheds its leaves. Hereinafter *roble* will be translated as oak, and *encino* as live oak.

15. Literally: The Pool of the Frogs. If the previous stop was near modern Crystal City, and if the direction now was east-northeast, this place was probably near present Brundage, Texas.

16. The Nueces river was probably crossed near present Palm, Texas.

17. The Spanish is *nogales.* The *nogal* is the common walnut (*Juglans sulcata*). José M. Ponce de León, *Datos Geográficos y Estadísticos del*

Estado de Chihuahua, p. 97, Chihuahua, 1907. The diarist undoubtedly confused the pecan, so prevalent in that region, with the walnut. Hereinafter the *nogal* is translated as pecan.

18. El Charco de Ranas.

19. The Resurrection. If the direction now is northeast, this may have been present Januey creek, near the spot where today Zavalla, Frio, Dimmit, and La Salle counties join.

20. Baltasar de Zúñiga, Marqués de Valero, thirty-sixth viceroy of New Spain. He was viceroy from August, 1716, to October, 1722. Gómez de la Puente (ed.), *Iconografía de Gobernantes de la Nueva España.*

21. La Resurrección.

22. *Hedionda* means stinking.

23. The Frio river may have been crossed near present Pearsall or Melon, Texas, or if the route lay farther to the northwest, it was probably crossed near modern Frio Town. If the dry creek referred to was the Leona river near present Divot, the first route may be the right one. However, since Alarcón later crossed a stream which the diarist calls Arroyo Hondo, one is led to believe that the second route is more plausible. Again the lack of directions makes it difficult to trace the route.

24. If the direction was northeast and since it was about two and a half leagues from the Arroyo Hondo, La Hedionda may have been on or near present Seco creek.

25. Probably the same stream that was named *Rio Hondo* (Deep river), on April 6, 1689, by De León on his expedition into Texas. West, "De León's Expedition," p. 208.

26. This may have been present Seco creek.

27. The Spanish is *una cuadra estrecha.* The meaning is not clear. It may mean that the creek ran straight for a distance of a street block (*cuadra*), about a quarter of a mile in those days, or that the creek ran through a narrow pass (*cuadra estrecha*) or ravine until it came out on the plain.

28. The Arroyo Hondo.

29. Literally: The Little Rush, probably because there were patches of reeds or rushes at this place. If the direction was northeast, this place may have been near present Devine or Natalia.

30. Literally: The Pools of the Century Plant. This place was probably in the vicinity of modern LaCoste or Macdona, Texas.

31. The stream received its name from a tribe of Indians living near it. See Introduction, note 30.

32. The full name was Fray Miguel Núñez de Aro. He was a signer of one of the affidavits found with the diary. See also Introduction, note 63.

33. See Introduction, note 4.

34. The lake known as Santa Ana or Las Cargas, mentioned by Pichardo. Hackett, *Pichardo's Treatise,* I, 339–340. See also Introduction,

note 63, and the entry for June 27. It seems, however, that the diarist made a mistake in regard to the date that the cargoes left the Rio Grande.

35. Probably the present Brazos. As will be noted later, Alarcón, like almost all the other Spanish explorers of Texas, called the present Brazos the Colorado. See entries for October 3d and 5th.

36. The creek of Los Payayas.

37. Named Medina by De León in 1689. West, " De León's Expedition," p. 209.

38. Reference is probably to the many cypress still common along the Medina and Guadalupe rivers.

39. From Aguayo's diary, Pichardo estimates the distance from the Presidio del Rio del Norte to the San Antonio river to be sixty-two leagues. Hackett, *Pichardo's Treatise,* I, 329. The total number of leagues traveled by Alarcón between the same points was sixty-three. Espinosa (*Chrónica Apostólica,* 450) states that the soldiers estimated the distance to be eighty leagues.

40. Evidently the same creek as that called Arroyo del León by the De León expedition of 1689 and which Miss West says was the San Antonio, probably in its upper reaches. " De León's Expedition," p. 210. If this be the case, Alarcón may have gone as far north as present Rio Medina, Texas, and then cut east. Father Tous believes that the arroyo called De León was the Leon Creek of today. " Ramón Expedition: Espinosa's Diary of 1716," p. 9, note 2.

41. Evidently San Pedro Springs in present San Antonio. It was given that name by the Ramón Expedition of 1716. *Ibid.,* p. 9; and Foik, " Domingo Ramón's Diary," p. 12.

42. Alarcón founded the villa of Bejar on May 5, 1718.

43. It is interesting to note that there is no entry from April 25th to May 5th. Perhaps the time was spent in finding suitable locations for the presidio, the mission, and the villa.

44. See Introduction, p. 23.

45. Present Cibolo creek, probably encountered near modern Selma, since from subsequent information we note that Alarcón went northeast. However, the distance seems too far. We may now reject Miss Buckley's statement that the name of this creek was first used in the Peña *Derrotero.* " Aguayo Expedition," pp. 35–36, note 1.

46. Present Salado creek, crossed probably near the present bridge on the Austin-San Antonio highway. The 1709 diary of Fathers Espinosa and Olivares speaks of an *arroyo salogre* (salty creek, the *salogre* probably being a mistake for *salobre*). In 1716, it was called Salado by Espinosa and Ramón. It is one of the few streams in Texas that kept the same name through all the expeditions that visited Texas. *Ibid.,* pp. 35–36, note 1; Foik, " Domingo Ramón's Diary," p. 12; Tous, " Ramón Expedition: Espinosa's Diary," p. 10.

47. Named in honor of the patron saint of Mexico, Nuestra Señora de Guadalupe. It was given this name in its lower reaches by De León in 1689. In 1691, Massanet and Terán crossed it about twelve leagues above present Gonzales, where it is joined by the San Marcos river, and Terán changed its name to San Agustín. In 1709, Fathers Espinosa and Olivares called it the Guadalupe. Espinosa and Ramón in 1716, and Peña in 1721, called the present Comal river the Guadalupe and the present Guadalupe the San Ybon. Buckley, "Aguayo Expedition," p. 36, note 1. By the "second river" of Guadalupe, Alarcón undoubtedly meant the modern Guadalupe, near present New Braunfels, Texas.

48. Literally: St. Michael's creek. This was possibly present Comal creek (as distinguished from the Comal river) near modern New Braunfels. Alarcón probably encountered it somewhere between present Dittlinger and New Braunfels. It is interesting to note that in 1727, Rivera called the present Comal river the San Miguel creek. Hackett, *Pichardo's Treatise*, I, 485.

49. The present Comal river near modern New Braunfels. At this place Comal creek runs into the Comal river near modern Landa Park.

50. The present Guadalupe river at modern New Braunfels.

51. The meaning is that the banks are too high and not that the water is too deep.

52. The Comal river joins the Guadalupe about a mile upstream from the bridge which crosses the Guadalupe on the present Austin-San Antonio highway at New Braunfels.

53. This may be the ford still used in present Landa Park at New Braunfels.

54. The present Rio Jamapa, state of Veracruz, Mexico. It empties into the Gulf of Mexico at the place where the first Veracruz was, about ten kilometers south of present Veracruz.

55. Literally: Get out if you can. This is the first time that directions are given, perhaps because the route was changed from northeast to east and southeast. If the directions are correct and if previously they were at present New Braunfels, Salsipuedes may have been near present Belmont, and Alarcón traveled parallel to the Guadalupe river. The distance is probably not correct because there were many detours, and a closer guess may be a spot near present Kingsbury, for the next entry states that they traveled another ten leagues, passing, at seven leagues, the San Marcos river.

56. Literally: Enter to see it. No directions are given, but the route was probably east-southeast. Ten leagues east from present Kingsbury would have placed them near modern Saturn, but this is in contradiction to the fact that at seven leagues the San Marcos river was encountered. The spot of Entraaverlo was then three leagues from the San Marcos, perhaps just north of present Gonzales.

57. Correctly written *cocolmécatl*, which means "twisted like a rope."

It is a bush, the branches of which were used for making cradles. The word is derived from *cocol* (radical of *coltic* or *cocolli,* meaning twisted) and from *mecatl* or *mecate* (meaning rope or lasso). Information received through Señor Vito Alessio Robles from Señor Mariano Rojas of the Departamento de Idioma Mexicano, Consultas, of the Museo Nacional in Mexico City; see also Rémi Siméon, *Dictionnaire de la Langue Nahuatl ou Mexicaine,* Paris, 1885.

58. The present San Marcos, from the description and leagues given, encountered probably between present Ottine and Slayden, Texas. However, it is not seventeen leagues (ten and seven) from present New Braunfels to the San Marcos river near modern Slayden. The discrepancy may be explained by many detours.

59. From the description that follows this seems to have been the confluence of the present San Marcos and Guadalupe rivers near modern Gonzales.

60. The diarist says that this was not the real San Marcos, although it was, because at that time it was thought that the San Marcos flowed into the Gulf. (See entry for April 13th.) The first expedition into the region of the Texas Indians, that of De León, gave the name of San Marcos to a river near the coast that is thought by some authorities to have been the present Colorado, while others are inclined to believe that it was the present Navidad river, and still others that it was the present Lavaca. The general belief of the Spaniards at this time was also that the San Marcos was the first river of any size that was passed after the Guadalupe on the way to the province of the Texas Indians. Thus the present San Marcos and the present Colorado were continually confused. Espinosa and Olivares in 1709, and Ramón and Espinosa in 1716, gave the San Marcos its present name. As will be noted at the end of the diary, Alarcón on his return from the Texas, named the modern San Marcos, Los Inocentes. This name was applied to it by Aguayo in 1721 and by Rivera in 1727. Buckley, " Aguayo Expedition," p. 37, note 1; Bolton, "Location of La Salle's Colony," p. 188; Hackett, *Pichardo's Treatise,* I, 480–497.

61. The diarist probably meant only to the junction of the two streams. The meaning is not clear, for he tells of retracing their steps, then going south, and in the next paragraph of continuing upstream.

62. Probably a spot on the San Marcos about a league and a half above its junction with the Guadalupe. On May 10th, they traveled six leagues in all. They spent four and a half leagues traveling from the place they arrived at on May 9th, and the remaining league and a half in retracing their steps to find the source of the San Marcos, *i.e.* upstream.

63. Evidently present Plum creek.

64. They probably reached a point between modern Fentress and Martindale.

65. The meaning is not clear, since they were on the river. The diarist probably meant the source of the river.

66. Unless they made many detours, it seems that this distance would have more than sufficed in bringing them to the crossing or even to the springs of the San Marcos river near modern San Marcos, Texas. The place reached is indefinite, but from later information it may be inferred that it was eight or nine leagues downstream from the ford near present San Marcos, or a point below modern Prairie Lea. See note 69.

67. Reference is to the expedition of Alonso de León of 1689. See West, "De León's Expedition," pp. 199–224; and Hackett, *Pichardo's Treatise,* I, 133–185.

68. The indefinite place referred to in note 65.

69. Perhaps the same ford used for many years on the Camino Real and which is found several miles below present San Marcos at a place locally known as the Stringtown community.

70. The indefinite place referred to in note 65. Eight or nine leagues downstream would put this place below present Prairie Lea.

71. Probably to a point near present Hunter, Texas.

72. Reference is to the Comal and Guadalupe rivers, at present New Braunfels, which Alarcón called the two branches of the Guadalupe.

73. The Edwards Plateau rises about half a league from the Guadalupe at New Braunfels. The springs of the present Comal river originate at the base of the escarpment here.

74. Probably to some place on the Guadalupe river between present Waco Springs and Sattler, in Comal county.

75. Probably the ford across the Guadalupe at present New Braunfels, which, until the recent construction of a dam just below this point, was still used locally.

76. As will be noted later, these were the top branches of a cypress, which were undoubtedly submerged by the flood, and were from time to time appearing on the surface.

77. The meaning is that the buttons of the pants at the waist came off, causing the pants to drop, and thus, since they were fastened at the knees, to form a serious impediment in the water.

78. That is, on May 16th, the day following the accident.

79. Fray Pedro Muñoz.

80. See Introduction, pp. 38–39.

81. Probably the present Brazos. See entries for October 3d and 5th.

82. There are no entries from June 27th to August 27th; in this time Alarcón must have returned to San Antonio.

83. Father Muñoz, who had been sent in search of the cargoes.

84. Fray Espinosa.

85. Reference is to Father Núñez and his company who left the cargo hidden near the Trinity. Núñez accompanied Muñoz in retrieving the supplies.

86. Domingo Ramón and Father Espinosa respectively.

87. The meaning is that an Indian was drowned in attempting to

cross the flooded streams in order to deliver to the missions of East Texas the letters left by Father Núñez when he had to turn back.

88. The villa of Bejar.

89. There are no entries from August 27th to September 3d.

90. The road was left about five or six miles south of modern New Braunfels.

91. The Guadalupe river must have been struck almost directly west of present Seguin, Texas.

92. The meaning is that the present Comal and Guadalupe rivers, which Céliz called the first branch and second branch of the Guadalupe, had joined above this spot.

93. Including the three before they left the road "which goes to Tejas."

94. In the Roman Catholic calendar September 8th is the day of the birth of the Virgin Mary.

95. The common prickly-pear cactus (*Opuntia vulgaris*) of the Texas prairies.

96. If the directions are right, the expedition passed along the south bank of the Guadalupe at modern Seguin, and stopped at a point east of Seguin on the Guadalupe or a little beyond.

97. The Moruame, or Muruam, tribe intermarried a good deal with a branch of the Tonkawa nation known as Ervipiame. After 1726 Muruam neophytes were included in the mission of San Antonio de Valero. Hodge, *Handbook*, I, 958.

98. Probably near present Belmont, Texas.

99. Probably near modern Monthalia.

100. Near present Gonzales, the junction they had encountered on their short expedition in May.

101. By the Guadalupe the diarist means the present Comal river, which until now he had called the first branch of the Guadalupe.

102. The present Guadalupe, called the Alarcón by the diarist probably because it was the stream in which Alarcón had his narrow escape from drowning.

103. The present San Marcos. The idea the diarist is trying to bring out is that at this junction really three rivers are running in one—the present Comal, Guadalupe, and San Marcos.

104. Probably near present Hamon, Texas.

105. Probably near present Hochheim, Texas.

106. The present Comal.

107. The present San Marcos.

108. This may have been either the present Blanco river or present Plum creek, both of which flow into the San Marcos. Rivera in his entry for June 21, 1727, says, "I spent the night of that day on the uninhabited Arroyo de San Rafael which others call the Blanco." Hackett, *Pichardo's Treatise*, I, 485–486. Miss Buckley is of the opinion that Rivera in 1727

(as well as Espinosa and Olivares in 1709, and Espinosa and Ramón in 1716) named present Plum creek the San Rafael. " Aguayo Expedition," p. 37, note 2.

109. Since they spent the whole day in crossing, this name was probably given to the place directly across the river from that named, on the preceding day, the Camp of the Most Holy Name of Mary.

110. Since, two paragraphs hence, the diarist with seeming emphasis says that the direction was northeast, we are fairly certain that in the present entry he meant that on the way they passed over some hills that were northeast from the place where they stopped that day, and that the expedition itself continued downstream. Therefore, if they continued downstream, they probably reached a place below present Cuero, Texas. On the other hand, if they had here begun to travel toward the northeast, the total number of leagues given until they reached the present Colorado river would have placed them far beyond that stream. Since the directions are not clear, and since we cannot rely on the distance given, owing to the fact that they were mere conjectures and that often the expedition became lost, had to return, and had to make many detours, we are not certain which bay on the coast they finally reached. From the distances and directions given, when stated, it seems that they reached present Matagorda bay, at some point on the peninsula that separates present Lavaca bay from Carancahua bay. The paragraphs describing the bay reached by Alarcón seem to confirm this assumption, since the bay is described as forming a semicircle running from north to southwest, that the present Colorado enters the bay toward the northeast, and that La Salle's colony had been established toward the west. See entries for September 23d and 24th.

111. Again no directions are given, but they probably continued downstream. If this be the case, they probably stopped near present Nursery.

112. Here the directions are definitely, and seemingly emphatically, given. The expedition probably stopped near present Salem, Texas.

113. Although there is a discrepancy in the date, the reference is evidently to the stigmatization on September 14, 1224, of St. Francis of Assisi, the founder of the order to which all the early missionaries in Texas belonged. St. Francis had gone up Mt. Alverno in the Apennines to fast and pray, and after forty days of contemplation, a vision of a seraph nailed upon a cross appeared to him and he was filled with joy. When the vision disappeared, he experienced pains and soon noticed on his body the " Stigmata of the Crucified," the five wounds of Christ on the cross. After this, cases of stigmatization occurred often, but usually only among members of the Franciscan or Dominican orders.

114. No directions are given, but they probably went northeast. If this be the case, and since five leagues were traveled, the last two streams they encountered were the present Lavaca and Navidad rivers, the one on

which they stopped being the Navidad, probably between present Gandy and Morales, Texas.

115. The present Colorado.

116. They probably reached the Colorado near present Garwood and Nada, Texas.

117. The present Colorado.

118. Probably to a point near present El Campo, Texas.

119. Literally: The Plain of St. Isidore.

120. The present Colorado, probably near modern Markham, Texas.

121. If our previous estimates have been correct, by now they could not go east-southeast without crossing the river, since for several leagues it has been running due south. Unless the river has greatly changed its course since those days, this was probably a mistake for west-southwest.

122. The meaning is not clear. If they started the day by going east-southeast, they should have been on the river. This changing of direction to the east-northeast may clarify the discrepancy suggested in the preceding note, and the expedition began this day's march by going west-south-west instead of east-southeast.

123. Probably to a point near present Beadle, Texas.

124. Again probably an error for southwest, because if the direction had been southeast, they would have immediately encountered the wide mouth of the Colorado which here runs due south, and, which, if it had been the inlet they soon thereafter discovered, they would have had to circle by crossing the river and not by going "four leagues to the south, the west, and in the direction of the north," as the diarist relates.

125. Probably modern Tres Palacios bay, encountered perhaps at a point almost directly opposite present Palacios, Texas.

126. Evidently present Carancahua bay, encountered possibly near the site of modern Carancahua, Jackson county, Texas.

127. If the previous estimates have been correct, the expedition probably went southeast on the peninsula which separates present Lavaca and Carancahua bays, and arrived on Matagorda bay, possibly at the southeast tip of the said peninsula and almost directly south and across the bay from present Carancahua.

128. Probably an error for southeast, since at the end of the paragraph the diarist says that the Colorado enters present Matagorda bay "on the other side of the aforementioned islet, which forms an angle with the bay." The "islet" was probably the small peninsula which extends into present Matagorda bay south of modern Collegeport, Matagorda county, Texas.

129. This description seems to confirm the assumption that the bay which the expedition reached and called Espíritu Santo was modern Matagorda bay.

130. The island referred to here may have been present Matagorda peninsula.

131. The channel referred to here seems to be the bay itself that the expedition encountered, *i.e.* present Matagorda bay.

132. It seems that the diarist called the two small inlets which the expedition circled on the preceding day, Todos Santos and San Bernardo. There was a great deal of confusion among the Spaniards as to which bays were called Todos Santos and San Bernardo, and this confusion was closely related to that concerning the question as to which bay was Espíritu Santo. By some Spaniards Espíritu Santo was thought to be the same as Todos Santos, while others were certain that Espíritu Santo was San Bernardo. An expedition headed by Francisco de Llanos in 1690 entered present Lavaca bay and named it Todos Santos. Captain Francisco Martínez, who accompanied the Terán expedition of 1691, named what seems to have been present Espíritu Santo bay, the Lago de Todos Santos. Although there was even greater confusion in regard to the bay of San Bernardo, it seems that the bay commonly known by that name by both French and Spaniards was present Matagorda bay. Bolton, "Location of La Salle's Colony," pp. 178, 179–180; Hackett, *Pichardo's Treatise,* I, 360, 381, note 1, 415, note 2, 418, 423–459, 464, note 3, 466, 469, note 3, 472, note 2, 533, note 2.

133. The present Colorado.

134. The mission of Peyotes was founded on December 13, 1698, and was first named Misión del Valle de San Bartolomé de Jesús. It was established between the Sabinas and Rio Grande rivers, about fifty leagues north of Monclova, Coahuila, and in the vicinity of the small range of mountains known as the Lomería de Peyotes. The name Peyotes is derived from a cactus very common to that district, which has medicinal and narcotic qualities and which, since it is also believed to have spiritual efficacy, is used by the Indians in their religious ceremonies. The mission of Peyotes was the poorest of the Coahuila missions, being sometimes without even a priest. Matías de la Mota Padilla, *Historia de la Conquista de la Provincia de la Nueva-Galicia,* p. 382, Mexico City, 1870; Manuel Orozco y Berra, *Geografía de las Lenguas y Carta Etnográfica de México,* pp. 302–303; Esteban L. Portillo, *Apuntes para la Historia Antigua de Coahuila y Texas,* pp. 273–277; Bancroft, *North Mexican States,* I, 607, note 9.

135. The Franciscan friars were divided into three branches which in Spanish received the following names: (1) "de la Observancia," including those of the "estrecha observancia," or strict observance, or "descalzos," barefooted; (2) the "Capuchinos," of which there never were any in Mexico; and (3) the "Conventuales," also lacking in Mexico. In Mexico those friars called "de la Observancia" were divided into five regular provinces or entities. The province of Santiago de Jalisco, to which Fray Céliz belonged, was the fourth of these provinces. Rev. Luis de Palacio to Sr. Vito Alessio Robles, February 11, 1933, MS., copies of which are in the University of Texas Library.

136. Espinosa and Domingo Ramón had brought along three Texas (Hasinai) Indians when they came in search of the supplies hidden in a wood. When, after their arrival at San Antonio, they decided to accompany Alarcón to Espíritu Santo bay and to East Texas, they took along the three Indians and used them as guides. Espinosa, *Chrónica Apostólica*, p. 451.

137. The Hasinai Indian guide; see preceding note.

138. Probably the same tribe as that also known as Coaque, Cadoque, Capoque, Cocos, Cokés, and Quoaquis. They were living on present Galveston island when Cabeza de Vaca was shipwrecked there in 1528 and may have been the same as the Koienkahé met by La Salle on Matagorda bay and mentioned by Joutel in 1687. They were a branch of the larger Karankawa (Carancahua) nation of coast Indians, named by Joutel *Korenkake* (of which Koienkahé may be a misprint). Hodge, *Handbook*, I, 315–316, 657–658.

139. Dr. Bolton has definitely located La Salle's ill-fated colony on modern Garcitas river, on the same site that Aguayo in 1722 built his fort of Nuestra Señora de Loreto. Bolton, " Location of La Salle's Colony," pp. 184, 188.

140. The present Colorado.

141. The present Colorado, according to our estimates (see note 116, above) at a place about four leagues upstream from present Garwood.

142. The Anames (Aranames, Hazanames, Juranames, Xaranames, or Arrenamuses) were a small agricultural tribe living on the southern coast of Texas. For a time they were residents of the mission of Espíritu Santo de Zúñiga, near present Goliad. In 1822 they were located on the San Antonio river. They were extinct as a tribe by 1843. La Salle, on his first journey from his Fort St. Louis, in 1686, visited an Indian village known as Anamis. Hodge, *Handbook*, I, 53, 72.

142a. The medlar, a small, generally bushy tree. Its botanical name is *Mespilus germanica;* it is related to the crab apple, being cultivated in gardens for its fruit. It is wild in central and southern Europe.

143. Reference is evidently to the Aname Indians.

144. There is a copy of this report in *Historia*, vol. 394, ff. 221–222, and in the Archivo del Convento Grande de San Francisco, B.N., photostat copies in the University of Texas Library, IX, 800–801. Alarcón stated in this report that he had left the villa of Bejar with ten families and a sufficient number of troops and that he did not have the thirty residents for his settlement because the Rio Grande was swollen and they could not be brought to San Antonio, especially not the women. He also asked that Olivares be given another missionary since he was alone, and yet had been granted two helpers, and since there were many Indians to be taught. In his trip to the coast he had crossed the best lands in the Indies, all of them level, fertile and with much water. He closed his report by stating that he was sending certificates to show that he had com-

plied with his orders, that he was on the point of leaving for the province of the Texas Indians, and that it might be well to send supplies to Texas by water as far as Espíritu Santo bay. On November 7th, an additional missionary was granted Olivares, but Alarcón's plans to send supplies to Espíritu Santo bay were abandoned. *Mandamiento del virrey,* November 7, 1718, MS., A.G.N., *Historia,* vol. 394, f. 223.

145. The present Colorado, crossed probably between modern Altair and Eagle Lake.

146. Probably modern San Bernard river northeast of present Eagle Lake.

147. Probably to some point just west of modern Sealy.

148. The Mayeyes, Malleyes, or Macheyes were one of the Tonkawan tribes. They roamed over almost all of present Texas west of the Trinity. About 1747, the San Xavier group of missions on the present San Gabriel river, near modern Georgetown, Texas, were founded for them among other tribes, the San Xavier region having always been the favored district of the Mayeyes. Hodge, *Handbook,* I, 824–825.

149. Since the next paragraph states that they stopped on a creek, this was probably present Mill creek near modern Bellville, Texas.

150. Possibly the same tribe as that known also as Paiugan, Payugan, Payuhuan, Pajuguan, and Payaguanes. It was probably a Coahuiltecan tribe. After 1703, they were at the mission of San Francisco Solano and when that mission became the mission of San Antonio de Valero, members of the tribe entered it. Payugan Indians were baptized there between 1720 and 1741. Rivera, in 1727, mentioned them as a Coahuila tribe. There is also a possibility that the Payugans were the same as the Paguan tribe met by Massanet on the road to the Texas Indians in 1690. From 1743 to 1748, a tribe known as Paguanan or Pahuanan was recorded at the mission of San Antonio de Valero. Hodge, *Handbook,* II, 184, 218.

151. See note 149. Terán in 1691 gave the present Brazos the name of San Gerónimo. Hackett, *Pichardo's Treatise,* I, 495.

152. Probably the same tribe as that known also as Sanas. See Introduction, note 31.

153. The Emet or Emat nation was met by De León and Massanet near the lower Guadalupe river in 1689. In 1690, De León encountered them on the east bank of the Colorado, living with the Cava, Too, and Toaa Indians. They did not speak the Coahuiltecan language, but it is not known whether they were of Tonkawan or Karankawan affiliation. Hodge, *Handbook,* I, 422, 657–658, II, 779.

154. The Too tribe was also known as Atayos, Tayos, Thoo, Tohan, Tohau, Toho, and Toxo. They were of Tonkawan affiliation, and associated with, but distinct from, the Tohaha. After 1740 the Too entered the San Antonio de Valero mission in considerable numbers. They were reported to have been in that mission until 1765. In later times they were

also known as Tou and Tuu. They were closely associated with the Cavas and the Emets. Hodge, *Handbook*, I, 422, II, 771, 779.

155. No definite information concerning this tribe has been found. There is a possibility that it was the same as that known as Camai, recorded at the San Antonio de Valero mission, or perhaps that its name is another spelling for Kariko or Korkone, which were merely two distinct ways of naming the Tonkawa nation. *Ibid.,* II, 426, 782–783.

156. Probably the direction was still north, and, owing to the great gathering of Indians, the expedition stopped just north of modern Bellville.

157. There is evidently a mistake in directions here, the correct direction being northwest, for if the expedition had traveled northeast, it would soon have reached the Brazos. It probably arrived on modern Yegua creek between present Independence and Clay.

158. The *tejocote* is a small yellow Mexican fruit belonging to the hawthorn family. The name is Aztec, the real spelling being *texócotl,* meaning wild acid fruit or hard acid fruit (from *tetl,* meaning rock, and *xocotl,* meaning acid fruit). The fruit is used against dropsy and its botanical name is *Pomum saxeum.* Information received through the courtesy of Señores Mariano J. Rojas and Juan E. Magallanes of the Departamento de Idioma Mexicano and Mrs. Bertha McKee Dobie, and by consulting Siméon, *Dictionnaire de la Langue Nahuatl ou Mexicaine,* p. 489.

159. The direction was probably more northwest than north, and the expedition arrived at some point near modern Cook's Point.

160. The Little river. The expedition evidently stopped at a place near present Gause, Milam county.

161. The present Brazos.

162. In the Roman Catholic calendar October 4th is the day of St. Francis of Assisi.

163. Undoubtedly the present Little river near its confluence with the Brazos.

164. The modern Brazos.

165. The present Brazos, crossed probably about one or two miles north of modern Sullivan, Milam county, and Good, Robertson county.

166. Rivera, in 1727, called a spot Los Angeles that was on the east bank of the Brazos at this point. Pichardo, using Rivera's *Derrotero,* gives the number of leagues from the junction of the Little river and the Brazos to Los Angeles as being two. Alarcón went seven leagues from a place half a league south of the Little river, so that the distance is about the same, since Alarcón crossed the Brazos above its junction with the Little river. The place of Los Angeles was probably at some point near modern Franklin. Hackett, *Pichardo's Treatise,* I, 335, 492.

167. A creek near the modern Navasota river, probably south of present Easterly, Texas. In 1716, Ramón and St. Denis reached a river not

far from the village of the Texas Indians, which they called Corpus Christi. Solís in 1768, reached a stream in this same region which he called Corpus Christi. Rivera, in 1727, traveling almost the same route that Alarcón took in this region, reached the creek of Corpus Christi eight leagues from the place called Los Angeles. *Ibid.*, I, 223, 335, 492, 529–530, 532.

168. The present Navasota river, crossed probably about five miles south of modern Ridge, Robertson county, and Dean, Leon county, Texas. Espinosa, in 1716, called the present Navasota the San Buenaventura. Aguayo, in 1721, gave it the same name. Buckley, " Aguayo Expedition," p. 41, note 1. Rivera in 1727, traveling approximately the same route as Alarcón at this point, states that he went six leagues from the Corpus Christi to the northeast, and " after having crossed the arroyo which they call Navasoto, I halted a short distance from it, by a lagoon of fresh water which is named Santa Ana." Hackett, *Pichardo's Treatise*, I, 530.

169. See the entry for April 21st, above. Pichardo, using Rivera's *Derrotero*, gives the distance from the creek of Corpus Christi to the lake of Santa Ana as six leagues, approximately the same as that given by the diary of Céliz. Hackett, *Pichardo's Treatise*, I, 335.

170. Probably near modern Centerville. Aguayo, in 1721, reached a place called Santa Clara at a distance of twelve leagues from the north bank of the lake of Santa Ana. *Ibid.*, I, 339–340.

171. Rivera gives the distance from Santa Ana lake to San Luis as eleven leagues. *Ibid.*, I, 335. The leagues between the two places as given by the diarist of the Alarcón expedition amount to fourteen. However, Rivera fails to mention the lake of San Christoval and thus may have traveled a different route at this point. The lake of San Luis Obispo and creek of Santa Rosa were probably near present Nineveh, Texas.

172. The Trinity river was probably reached and crossed at a point between present Malvern, Leon county, and Reynard, Houston county.

173. A *braza* was equal to six feet and was called by that name because it signified the length of both arms (*brazos*) extended.

174. Unless the Trinity river was farther west in those days, the expedition, by traveling twelve leagues toward the east-northeast, should have reached the Neches river. It is interesting to note that on Aguayo's route the distance from the place where he crossed the Trinity to Santa Coleta was also twelve leagues, whereas Rivera's distance between the two points was approximately eleven leagues. Hackett, *Pichardo's Treatise*, I, 335–336, 340.

175. Reference is to the mission of San Francisco de los Texas; see Introduction, note 9. Alarcón's distance from where he crossed the Trinity to the site of the former mission of San Francisco de los Texas in the valley of San Pedro, was sixteen leagues. Aguayo's and Rivera's distances between the same places were each fifteen leagues. Hackett, *Pichardo's Treatise*, I, 335–336, 340.

176. Reference is to Ramón's entry in 1716. It seems that this presidio had three locations. Miss Buckley believes that the place where the presidio "stood the first time" refers to "Ramón's leaving his soldiers just this side of the Neches while he and the missionaries went ahead to look for a site for the second San Francisco mission he was about to establish." "Aguayo's Expedition," pp. 43–44, note 4. The second location of the presidio, referred to by Pichardo in stating the distances of Aguayo's expedition, was probably also only a temporary camp of the soldiers of Ramón at or near the mission of San Francisco de los Texas, at the place where he reëstablished it in 1716. Hackett, *Pichardo's Treatise*, I, 340. The soldiers probably remained in camp near this mission until Ramón and the friars established the mission of Purísima Concepción. The permanent (or third) location of the presidio was about one league east of the mission of Concepción. See also Introduction, note 24.

177. Evidently the Neches river, crossed probably north of modern Weches.

178. Reference is to the mission of San Francisco de los Texas, re-founded in 1716 by Ramón. See Introduction, note 17.

179. See Introduction, note 2.

180. Reference is to the distance from La Coleta creek to the mission of San Francisco de los Texas, in the place where it was refounded by Ramón in 1716. If the distance from La Coleta to the plain of San Pedro is four leagues, as Alarcón's diarist says it is, then the distance from La Coleta to the mission of San Francisco as given by Rivera is nine leagues. Hackett, *Pichardo's Treatise*, I, 335–336. Aguayo gives the distance from La Coleta to the mission of San Francisco also as nine leagues. *Ibid.*, I, 340. The discrepancy of Alarcón's diarist may perhaps be explained by the number of leagues lost in looking for the spot where "in the entrance of the year '16 the presidio stood for the first time."

181. Doubtless the Angelina river, crossed west of modern Douglas, Nacogdoches county.

182. Reference is to the mission of Nuestra Señora de la Purísima Concepción. See Introduction, note 18.

183. Espinosa and Ramón went on ahead on October 12th. See entry for that date, above.

184. The mission was less than half a league from the Angelina river. Hackett, *Pichardo's Treatise*, I, 341.

185. The distance given by Aguayo from the mission of San Francisco to the presidio one league east of the mission of Concepción, was nine leagues. Hackett, *Pichardo's Treatise*, I, 340–341.

186. Alarcón.

187. This name was probably given by Alarcón to the settlement at the mission of Purísima Concepción.

188. Reference is evidently to the settlement at the mission of San

Joseph de los Nazones, and Alarcón probably gave it the name of Pueblo de San Joseph de Ayamonte. See entry for October 31st, below.

189. Reference is to the Cadodachos. See Introduction, note 41.

190. The Cadodachos at this time were probably still living among the lakes of northwestern Louisiana.

191. Espinosa's *Chrónica Apostólica*, p. 451, cited by Buckley, verifies this point, saying that the Indians "fired off more guns than all the Spaniards put together." Espinosa had counted ninety-two guns in the Indians' possession in the mission of Concepción, his headquarters. "Aguayo's Expedition," p. 7.

192. Possibly the Indian woman named Angelina or Angelique, in whose honor the Angelina river was probably named. Buckley, "Aguayo Expedition," p. 42, note 5.

193. An affidavit signed by the missionaries of East Texas, dated November 25, 1718, states that Alarcón was received as *Caddi Assinai* by the Indians, a term meaning chief of the Asinais or Texas. MS., A.G.N., *Tierras*, vol. 360.

194. The Bidais (Vidais or Beadeyes) were a tribe of Indians, probably of Caddoan stock, that had villages scattered over a large territory but chiefly along the Trinity river. Some of them reached as far north as the Neches and even beyond. They were neighbors and probably allies of the Arkokisa Indians on the lower Trinity. Toward the end of the eighteenth century the Bidai were the intermediaries between the French and the Apaches in the trade of firearms. They were a settled, agricultural tribe. In 1805, they numbered about one hundred and were said to be of excellent character as far as honesty and punctuality were concerned. Toward the middle of the nineteenth century a few survivors of the Bidai were living about twelve miles from Montgomery, Texas, where they cultivated the soil and worked as cotton pickers. The survivors of this last group were probably incorporated in the Caddo. *Bidai* is a Caddo word meaning brushwood. Hodge, *Handbook*, I, 145–146.

195. See Introduction, note 19.

196. In mining circles the word *quemazón* (meaning a big fire) is used to designate volcanic rock. Information received through the courtesy of Ing. Emilio Mosonyi, mining engineer of Mexico City.

197. Reference is to the relations between France and Spain. In the next year, 1719, the two countries went to war over European troubles, and the French from Louisiana attacked the East Texas settlements of the Spanish, causing the latter to be abandoned until 1721, when Aguayo reëstablished the missions there. For a more detailed account of the attack see Buckley, "Aguayo Expedition," pp. 8–20.

198. This is clearly a mistake for southeast, for the mission of Guadalupe de los Nacogdoches lay southeast of Purísima Concepción. It is interesting to note that the Peña *Derrotero* of the Aguayo expedition makes the same mistake, giving the direction as east-northeast. Rivera in 1727 gave the direction as east. *Ibid.,* p. 49, note 1.

199. Reference is to the mission of Nuestra Señora de Guadalupe de los Nacogdoches. See Introduction, note 20.

200. The settlement was probably given this name in honor of Francisco Fernández de la Cueva, Duque de Alburquerque, Marqués de Cuellar, viceroy of New Spain from 1702 to 1711.

201. A *representación* made July 22, 1716, by the fathers of the East Texas missions, gives the distance from Concepción mission to the mission of Guadalupe as eight leagues. MS., A.G.N., *Historia,* vol. 27, f. 209. The diary of the Aguayo expedition gives the distance to Nacogdoches from the presidio one league east of Concepción as eight leagues. Buckley, "Aguayo Expedition," p. 49, note 1.

202. The "same" direction would have been northeast, which is a mistake for east-southeast. See also the statement made by Miss Buckley in regard to the same error made by the diary of the Aguayo expedition of 1721. *Ibid.,* p. 49, note 5.

203. Aguayo, in 1721, arrived at a river named Todos Santos, fourteen leagues from the mission of Nuestra Señora de Guadalupe de los Nacogdoches. Pichardo believes that it was the same river which Rivera, in 1727, called the Atoyaque, a Mexican word meaning "in the river." Hackett, *Pichardo's Treatise,* I, 398–400. Miss Buckley believes that the Todos Santos was the Amoladero and not the Atoyaque or Attoyac. "Aguayo Expedition," p. 49, note 5.

204. The distance between the Nacogdoches mission and Todos Santos river, as given by the diary of the Aguayo expedition, was fourteen leagues. The distance as given by Rivera, in 1727, was thirteen leagues. Hackett, *Pichardo's Treatise,* I, 336, 341.

205. Reference is to the mission of Nuestra Señora de los Dolores de los Ais. See Introduction, note 22.

206. Pichardo, using Rivera's data of 1727, says the river of Todos Santos "is encountered some six leagues before reaching the mission of Los Ayx, situated near the Rio de Sabinas." Hackett, *Pichardo's Treatise,* I, 399.

207. This is the first time mention is made of Father Antonio Margil de Jesús. See Introduction, note 16.

208. See Introduction, note 22.

209. This statement does not agree with that made by Solís, in 1768, when he said that after fifty years of service, the mission records showed only eleven baptisms. Hodge, *Handbook,* I, 449, II, 94.

210. Reference is to the distance between the river of Todos Santos and the mission of Dolores de los Ais. This corresponds to the distances given by Aguayo and Rivera. Hackett, *Pichardo's Treatise,* I, 336, 342, 399.

211. Reference is to the discussion of what might be "necessary for the welfare of the province." See preceding paragraph.

212. From the distances given, this could not have been the present

Sabine river, since from the mission of Dolores de los Ais to the stream which Alarcón named San Francisco de Sabinas, about twenty leagues were covered. In regard to this point, it is interesting to note that unlike most of the entries in the diary, that for November 8th (the entry immediately preceding this one) does not have the number of leagues repeated in the margin of the manuscript. It may be that the person who put down the marginal annotations of the leagues for each entry noted the discrepancy and failed to put the number of leagues in the margin at this point. Furthermore, the distance given by Aguayo, in 1721, between the mission of Los Ais and the Rio de Sabinas was eleven leagues, a much closer estimate. Rivera's distance between the two points was fourteen leagues. Hackett, *Pichardo's Treatise*, I, 336, 342.

213. See Introduction, note 23.

214. This settlement was probably also named in honor of Francisco Fernández de la Cueva, Duque de Alburquerque, Marqués de Cuellar, viceroy of New Spain from 1702 to 1711.

215. According to the diarist, the distance traveled from Dolores de los Ais to San Miguel de los Adaes total forty-two leagues. Aguayo, in 1721, covered only thirty-two and three-quarter leagues between the two points. Rivera, in 1727, estimated the distance at thirty-two leagues. It is impossible that the great discrepancy could have occurred because of detours made by Alarcón's expedition. Even the distances given by the diaries of the Aguayo and Rivera expeditions are far too long, but Rivera must have gone too far north and had to retrace his steps, for in one of his entries, just before reaching San Miguel de los Adaes, he gives the direction as "east, a quarter to the southeast." Hackett, *Pichardo's Treatise*, I, 336, 342.

216. Natchitoches, Louisiana.

217. Probably the lagoon of Los Adaes (present Spanish Lake), near which, in 1721, Aguayo reëstablished the mission of San Miguel de los Adaes and established the presidio of Nuestra Señora del Pilar de los Adaes. Buckley, "Aguayo Expedition," p. 52.

218. The Red river near Natchitoches. See latter part of this entry and Hackett, *Pichardo's Treatise*, I, 402.

219. The villages of the Cadodacho Indians, at this time still inhabiting the region around the lakes of northwestern Louisiana. See Introduction, note 41.

220. The meaning here is ambiguous. It may be that the friars remonstrated against the idea of telling the French to move, a very possible suggestion, or that they remonstrated that the orders of the viceroy were not against hinting to the French that they leave Natchitoches, an entirely opposite interpretation. Alarcón later said that the religious restrained him from attacking the French and that the missionaries used his orders from the viceroy to reinforce their arguments for not making the attack against the French. He later lamented not having attacked the

French and also that his orders were not secret, so that he could have acted without asking the missionaries' advice. *Capítulo del tanto de la Consulta*, MS., A.G.N., *Historia*, vol. 394, ff. 224 (vuelta)–225; Alarcón to the king, November 3, 1721, MS., A.G.N., *Historia*, vol. 394, ff. 240–241. On the other hand, Espinosa, who was with Alarcón in East Texas at the time, said that if Alarcón had followed the orders of the viceroy, the French would not have attacked the East Texas settlements the next year, meaning evidently that Alarcón should have attacked them first. Espinosa, *Chrónica Apostólica*, p. 451.

221. The meaning is that the governor filled in the squad of twenty-five men under the command of Captain Domingo Ramón in East Texas. Of this squad seven were missing for various reasons, and for these, seven more were substituted in order to bring the squad to the required number of twenty-five. The original military escort of Domingo Ramón's expedition consisted of Domingo Ramón, his son and Lieutenant Diego Ramón, and twenty-two soldiers, a total of twenty-five men. Ramón diary, *Provincias Internas*, vol. 181, f. 31, *Historia*, vol. 27, f. 181 (vuelta); Espinosa, *Chrónica Apostólica*, p. 451; Clark, *Beginnings of Texas*, p. 64.

222. Reference is to the settlement at the mission of San Francisco de los Tejas at the site where it was established in 1690 by De León and Father Massanet. The Nabedache Indian village and the stream near which the mission was founded were known by the Spaniards as San Pedro or San Pedro de los Nabedaches (Navidachos). Hodge, *Handbook*, II, 436.

223. An *arroba* is approximately twenty-five pounds.

224. This description indicates that Alarcón was traveling with a certain degree of luxury.

225. The present Brazos.

226. Literally: great wood. From the directions given, the *monte grande* must have been northeast of present Brushy creek (Las Animas). Rivera in 1727 crossed the *monte grande* about two leagues northeast from the lower reaches of Brushy creek. Hackett, *Pichardo's Treatise*, I, 335.

227. Miss Buckley has identified this stream with present Brushy creek, the name Las Animas being given to it by Espinosa in 1716. Aguayo, in 1721, and Rivera, in 1727, gave it the same name. Buckley, "Aguayo Expedition," pp. 38–39, note 1.

228. The present Colorado.

229. It is not clear what the diarist means by passing the present Colorado in three branches. It seems improbable that Alarcón should have thought that he was encountering the present San Marcos, which he referred to, below modern Gonzales, as flowing in three branches, since immediately hereafter he crossed the present San Marcos, called it Los Inocentes, and then crossed the present Guadalupe and Comal rivers.

230. Present Onion creek, south of modern Austin. It received this

name in 1709 from Espinosa and Olivares who were bothered by ticks (*garrapatas*) while on this stream. In 1716, Espinosa gave it the same name, and Aguayo, in 1721, and Rivera, in 1727, also called it the Garrapatas. Buckley, " Aguayo Expedition," p. 38, note 2.

231. Probably the present Blanco river, a few miles north of modern San Marcos. See note 108.

232. The present San Marcos.

233. It is interesting to note that the name Los Inocentes was applied to the San Marcos by Aguayo in 1721 and by Rivera in 1727. Buckley, " Aguayo Expedition," p. 37, note 1; Hackett, *Pichardo's Treatise,* I, 334, 337, 485.

234. The springs of the San Marcos river are near the present highway between Austin and San Marcos, about a mile northeast of the latter place.

235. The present Guadalupe, near modern New Braunfels. See note 102.

236. See entry for May 16, above.

237. The present Comal at New Braunfels.

238. Reference is undoubtedly to the springs of the Comal river in present Landa Park at New Braunfels.

239. Reference is to the Jarame Indians, one of the chief tribes for whom Father Olivares wanted to establish a mission on the San Antonio river. See Introduction, note 29.

240. Very little is known of the Pamaya tribe. They were associated with the Sijame, Payayas, and Jarames. Members of the tribe were baptized at the mission of San Antonio de Valero and were also found among the tribes of the Ranchería Grande. Hodge, *Handbook,* II, 354, 426, 569.

241. Reference is to Louis de St. Denis. See Introduction, note 25.

242. The Ranchería Grande, or Large Village, was an extensive collection of Indian tribes and parts of tribes, found during the early part of the eighteenth century near the middle Brazos river in Texas. The natives of the region were probably Ervipiame, and to these were added fleeing apostates from the Spanish missions, Indian culprits sought by Spanish authorities, and parts of broken-up tribes. Like the Ervipiame, most of the Indians of the settlement were Tonkawan. The Ranchería Grande is mentioned as early as 1707 by Captain Diego Ramón of the presidio of San Juan Bautista on the Rio Grande. In 1716, it was above the present town of Cameron, Texas, and contained about 2,000 Indians. Hodge, *Handbook,* II, 354.

243. The meaning here is not clear, for Olivares arrived at San Antonio on May 1st, but it may mean that he had made a trip and returned during this interval to San Antonio.

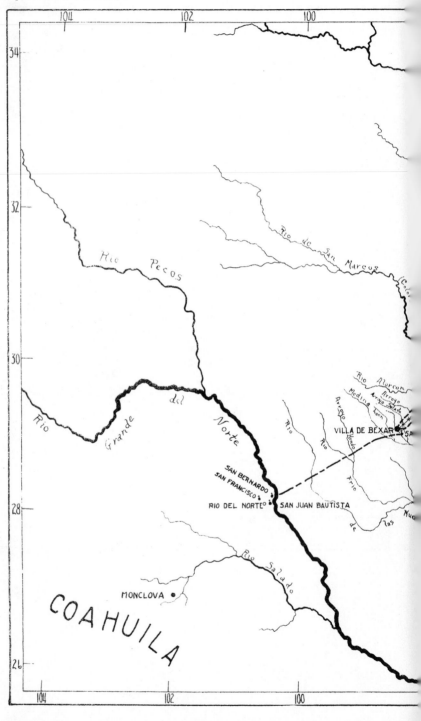

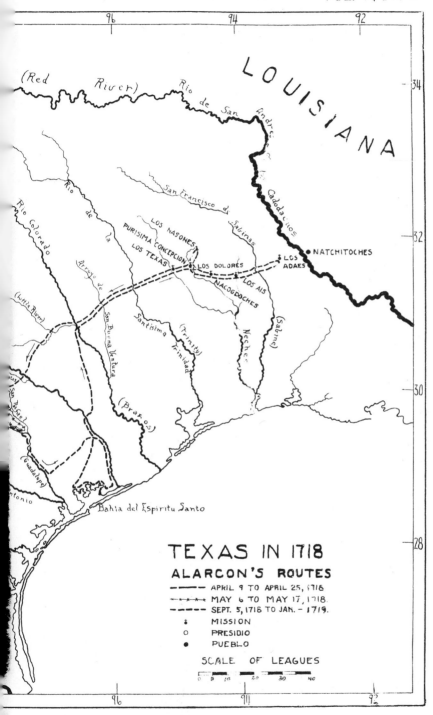

(Red River)
Rio de San Andres
LOUISIANA
Rio de la
Rio Colorado
San Francisco de
Sabinas
Cadodachos
NATCHITOCHES
LOS NASONES
PURISIMA CONCEPCION
LOS TEXAS
LOS DOLORES
LOS ADAES
Arroyo de
NACOGDOCHES
LOS AIS
(Little River)
San Buena Ventura
Santisima
(Trinity)
Trinidad
Neches
(Sabine)
(Brazos)
(Guadalupe)
ntonio
Bahia del Espiritu Santo

TEXAS IN 1718
ALARCON'S ROUTES
- - - - - APRIL 9 TO APRIL 25, 1718
+ + + + + MAY 6 TO MAY 17, 1718.
- - - - - SEPT. 5, 1718 TO JAN. - 1719.
⚹   MISSION
o   PRESIDIO
●   PUEBLO

SCALE OF LEAGUES

INDEX

Acuña. See *Concepción, Mission of Nuestra Señora de la Purísima*

Adaes Indians, 36

Adaes, Los, lake of. See *Los Adaes Lake*

Adaes, mission of. See *San Miguel de los Adaes*

Adaes, presidio of Nuestra Señora del Pilar de los, 33

Adays. See *Adaes*

Agreda. See *Concepción de Agreda*

Agriculture, begun at San Antonio, 55, 86. See *Irrigation*

Aguayo, San Miguel de, establishes presidio of Los Adaes, 33; presents gifts to Sana Indians, 35; refounds missions of San Miguel de los Adaes, 33, Ais, 32, Concepción, 31, Nacogdoches, 32, San José de los Nazones, 31

Aijado Indians, 6

Ais Indians, mission founded among, 32–33

Ais, mission of Nuestra Señora de los Dolores de los, Alarcón reaches, 80; founded, 14; history of, 32–33; mentioned, 107

Alamo. See *San Antonio de Valero*

Alarcón, Francisco de, son of Martín de Alarcón, 2

Alarcón, Martín de, appointed governor, 18, 36; appointed to lead expedition, 17–18; at Monclova, 20; at the Rio Grande, 20; begins expedition, 23, 43; cited, 41; confers with missionaries, 58, 80–81; conflict with missionaries, 23–25, 27, 82–83, 108–109; denied permission to visit Mexico City, 26; departure from Coahuila lamented, 26; descends Guadalupe river, 50–51, 59–62; detained by floods, 26, 85; duties of, 21–23; early life of, 19; estimate of work, 26–27; examines Espíritu Santo bay, 25; final instructions for, 21; founds mission of San Antonio de Valero, 23, 24, 49; founds Villa de Bexar, 23, 49, 93; given thanks, 26; governor of Coahuila, 19; in East Texas, 26, 70–84; in Mexico City, 19, 26; instructions for, 18–19, 21–23, 45; investigates St. Denis' activities, 20, 87; later life, 26; leaves East Texas, 84; leaves for East Texas, 25–26, 58; lies on snake, 64; meets Xanac nation, 35; named *Caddi Assinai,* 106; named *Cadi A Ymat,* 78; escapes drowning, 53–55, 96; orders seizure of French goods, 20; received by Texas Indians, 74, 75–76, 78; receives Espinosa and Domingo Ramón, 25, 56; receives instructions, 40; learns of St. Denis' escape, 34; recruits men, 20, 24; remuneration of, 38; renders *consulta,* 26; relieved from office, 26; reports to viceroy, 67–68, 84, 101; requests to viceroy, 26, 41; returns to San Antonio, 26, 86; returns to Rio Grande, 55–56; salary of, 19; sends supplies, 21, 38–39, 56; in Coahuila, 20; title of, 18

Alarcón river. See *Guadalupe river*

Alburquerque, Duque de. See *Cuellar, Marqués de*

Alburquerque, pueblo of. See *Nuestra Señora de Guadalupe de Alburquerque*

Alcalde mayor, Alarcón named to office of, 19

III